DRAW

COMIC BOOK CHARACTERS

BOOK HOUSE

SALARIYA

Published in Great Britain in MMXIII by
Book House, an imprint of
The Salariya Book Company Ltd
25 Marlborough Place, Brighton BN1 1UB

1 3 5 7 9 8 6 4 2

Please visit our website at **www.salariya.com**
for **free** electronic versions of:
You Wouldn't Want to Be an Egyptian Mummy!
You Wouldn't Want to Be a Roman Gladiator!
You Wouldn't Want to be a Polar Explorer!
You Wouldn't Want to sail on a 19th-Century Whaling Ship!

Authors:

Mark Bergin was born in Hastings in 1961.
He studied at Eastbourne College of Art and has
specialised in historical reconstructions as well as aviation
and maritime subjects since 1983. He lives in
Bexhill-on-Sea with his wife and three children.

David Antram was born in Brighton, England, in 1958. He
studied at Eastbourne College of Art and then worked in
advertising for fifteen years before becoming a full-time artist.
He has illustrated many children's non-fiction books.

Editor: Rob Walker

PB ISBN: 978-1-908759-67-2

A CIP catalogue record for this
book is available from the
British Library.

Printed and bound in China.
Printed on paper from
sustainable sources.

PAPER FROM
SUSTAINABLE
FORESTS

**WARNING: Fixatives should be
used only under adult supervision.**

@bookhousebooks   The Salariya   BookHouse100
                  Book Company

FIND OUR BOOKS
ON THE APP STORE:
SEARCH FOR 'SALARIYA'

Visit our **new** online shop at
shop.salariya.com
for great offers, gift ideas, all our new releases
and free postage and packaging.

I ✓

Contents

Drawing materials

Try using different types of drawing papers and materials. Experiment with charcoal, wax crayons and pastels. All pens, from felt-tips to ballpoints, will make interesting marks — try drawing with pen and ink on wet paper for a variety of results.

Silhouette is a style of drawing that uses only a solid black shadow.

Ink

Felt-tip

Charcoal is very soft and can be used for big, bold drawings. Ask an adult to spray your charcoal drawings with fixative to prevent smudging.

You can create special effects in a drawing done with **wax crayons** by scraping parts of the colour away.

6

Hard **pencil** leads are greyer and soft pencil leads are blacker. Hard pencils are graded from 6H (the hardest) through 5H, 4H, 3H and 2H to H. Soft pencils are graded from B, 2B, 3B, 4B and 5B up to 6B (the softest).

Pencil

Ink

Pastels are even softer than charcoal, and come in a wide range of colours. Ask an adult to spray your pastel drawings with fixative to prevent smudging.

Lines drawn in ink cannot be erased, so keep your ink drawings sketchy and less rigid. Don't worry about mistakes as these lines can be lost in the drawing as it develops.

7

Perspective

DRAW

If you look at a figure from different viewpoints, you will see that whichever part is closest to you looks larger, and the part furthest away from you looks smallest. Drawing in perspective is a way of creating a feeling of depth — of suggesting three dimensions on a flat surface.

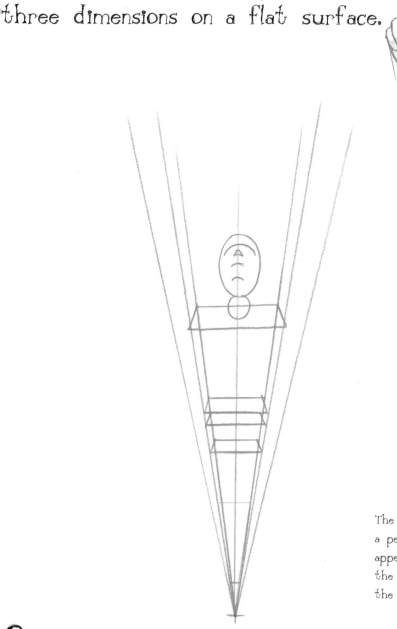

V.P.

The vanishing point (V.P.) is the place in a perspective drawing where parallel lines appear to meet. The position of the vanishing point depends on the viewer's eye level.

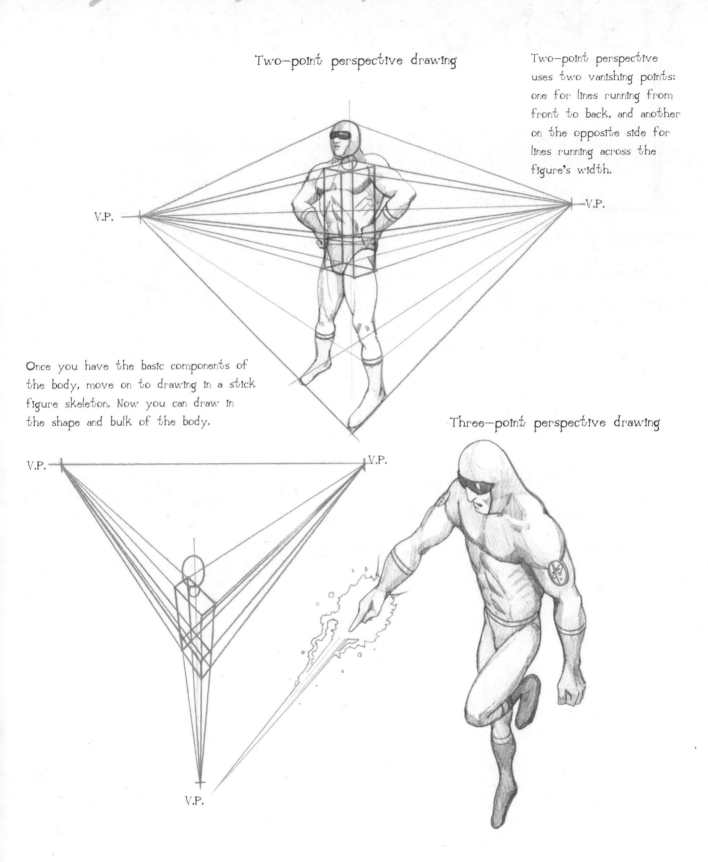

Two–point perspective drawing

Two–point perspective uses two vanishing points: one for lines running from front to back, and another on the opposite side for lines running across the figure's width.

V.P.

V.P.

Once you have the basic components of the body, move on to drawing in a stick figure skeleton. Now you can draw in the shape and bulk of the body.

Three–point perspective drawing

V.P.

V.P.

V.P.

Three–point perspective drawings use three vanishing points. This method is good for drawing objects at more dramatic angles.

V.P. = vanishing point

Making a start

DRAW

Learning to draw is about looking and seeing. Keep practising and get to know your subject. Use a sketchbook to make quick drawings. Start by doodling and experimenting with shapes and patterns. There are many ways to draw but this book shows only some methods. Visit art galleries, look at artists' drawings and see how your friends draw, but above all, find your own way.

You can practise drawing figures using an artist's model — a wooden figure that can be put into various poses.

When drawing from photos, use construction lines to help you to understand the form of the body and how each of its parts relate to each other.

Practice sketching people in everyday surroundings. This will help you to draw faster and train you to capture the main elements of a pose quickly.

Try sketching friends and family at home.

You can create new poses by drawing simple stick figures.

Character proportions

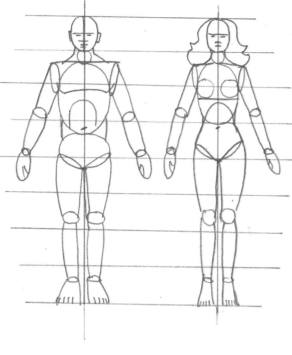

This page shows some of the more popular fantasy figures and their proportions compared to a normal human figure. On average, the length of a human head should fit eight times into its body length. When you draw a fantasy figure anything goes — so let your imagination go wild.

Draw these simple figures to
help you choose a good
position for your character.
You can emphasise the qualities
of a character by using
dramatic poses or emotions.

Adapting characters

These simple figures can be adapted to become any costumed hero striking a heroic pose. Here they can be seen as spies, sci—fi warriors or super heroes.

Spies

Using the basic figure, draw in the hands, hair and facial details. Then add the details of the spies' costumes and accessories.

Draw the basic shape of the figures using simple lines and ovals.

Draw a bag slung round the shoulder and hanging at waist level.

Add hi—tech glasses and microphones

Draw in the belt with pouches.

Using curved lines draw a long coat on the lady spy.

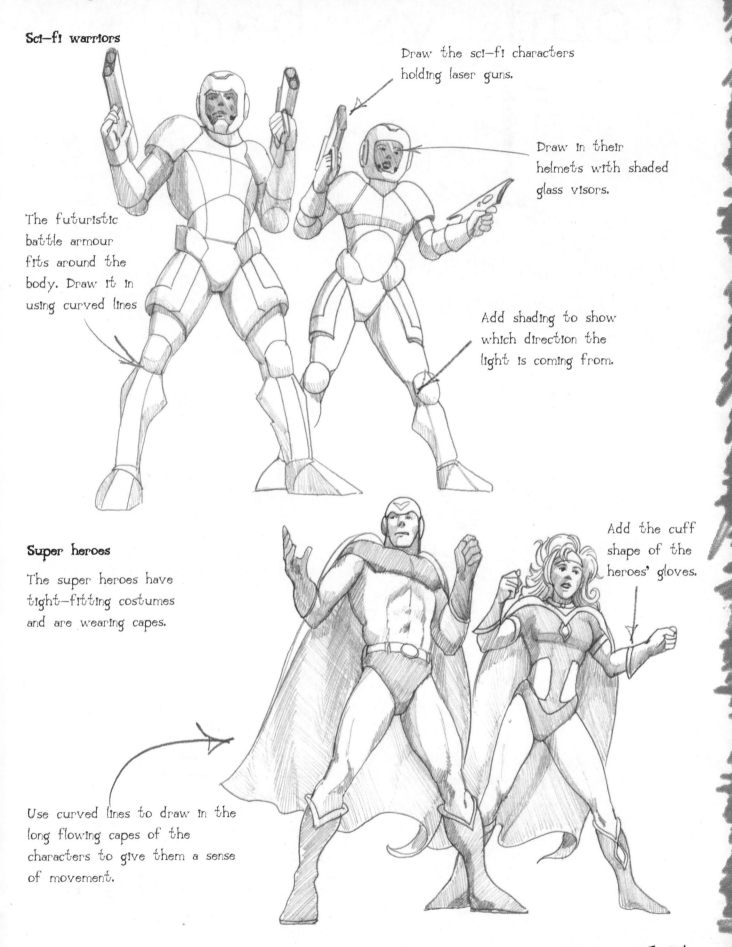

Sci-fi warriors

Draw the sci-fi characters holding laser guns.

Draw in their helmets with shaded glass visors.

The futuristic battle armour fits around the body. Draw it in using curved lines

Add shading to show which direction the light is coming from.

Super heroes

The super heroes have tight-fitting costumes and are wearing capes.

Add the cuff shape of the heroes' gloves.

Use curved lines to draw in the long flowing capes of the characters to give them a sense of movement.

15

Good vs bad

Every super hero needs a super villain to battle against! The details of a character's face and costume can instantly place them on the side of good or evil.

Here are some pretty evil character designs.

This set of super villains look ready to do evil. Note their rough and menacing appearance with torn, ragged capes and unfriendly looks.

The super heroes' looks are quite the opposite to that of the villains. They look clean and virtuous.

In this action scene the hero fights the villain. The villain's immense size helps to create a sense of intimidation and the scale of evil that must be overcome.

The hero is using his super powers to throw energy bolts at the villain.

Add in details like hair and bindings, and any costumes.

Try to capture the sense of movement in your drawings with the use of dramatic poses.

This dynamic pose shows the hero dealing out justice to a super villain scientist.

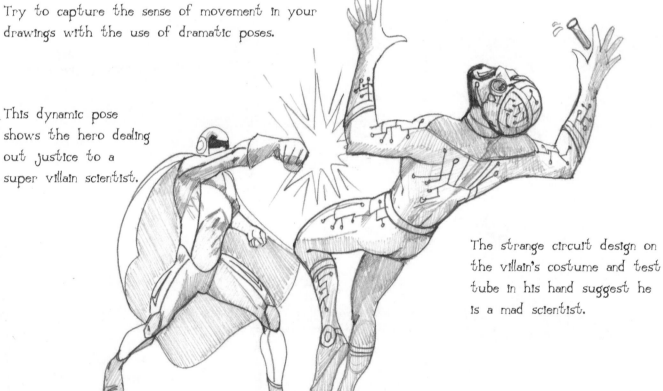

The strange circuit design on the villain's costume and test tube in his hand suggest he is a mad scientist.

Use perspective to add to the drama of the scene.

Running man

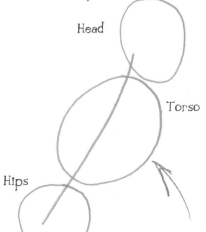

The running man uses his power of super speed to rescue those in peril and catch the villains.

Draw a straight line for the spine.

Head

Torso

Hips

Add three ovals: one each for the head, torso and hips. The torso oval is much longer.

Draw small circles for the shoulders.

Sketch in two cylinders to show the direction of the arms.

Draw in a large ellipse for each thigh.

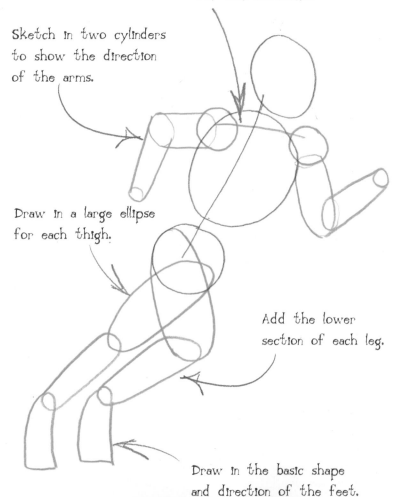

Add the lower section of each leg.

Draw in the basic shape and direction of the feet.

Action poses

Drawing basic stick figures can help you decide on a character's pose and what they might be doing.

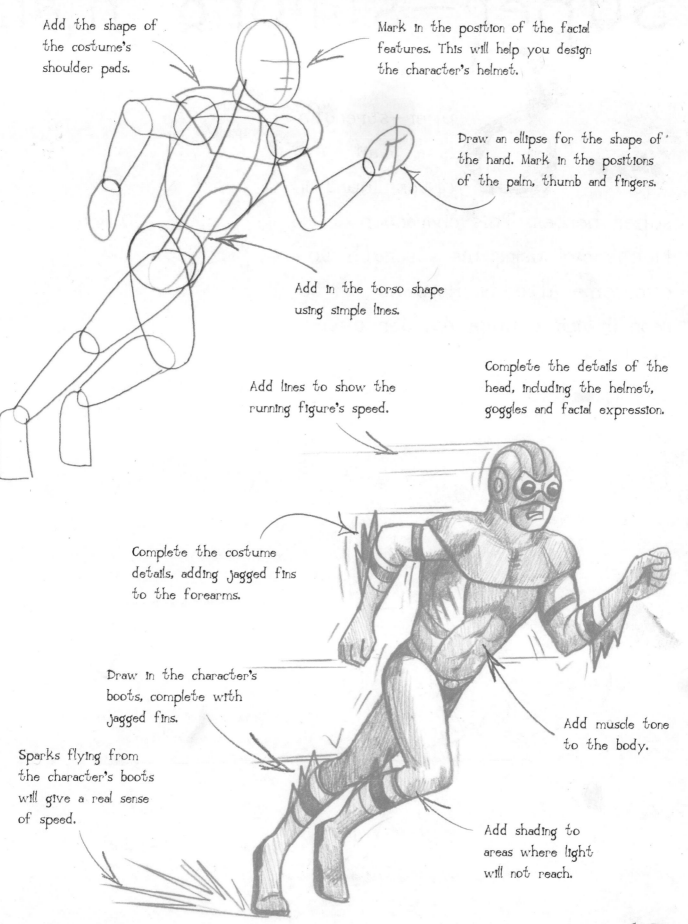

Add the shape of the costume's shoulder pads.

Mark in the position of the facial features. This will help you design the character's helmet.

Draw an ellipse for the shape of the hand. Mark in the positions of the palm, thumb and fingers.

Add in the torso shape using simple lines.

Add lines to show the running figure's speed.

Complete the details of the head, including the helmet, goggles and facial expression.

Complete the costume details, adding jagged fins to the forearms.

Draw in the character's boots, complete with jagged fins.

Sparks flying from the character's boots will give a real sense of speed.

Add muscle tone to the body.

Add shading to areas where light will not reach.

DRAW Super-strong man

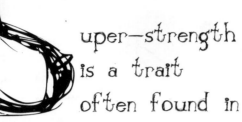

Super-strength is a trait often found in super heroes. This character fights evil using his strength to overcome all odds. Here he can be seen lifting a huge boulder over his head.

Draw in a straight line for the character's spine.

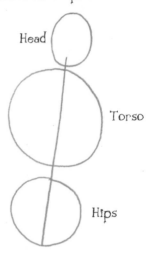

Head

Torso

Hips

Add three circles for the head, torso and hips. Make the torso shape larger.

Add a small circle for each shoulder.

Add powerful thighs coming out from the hip circle.

Draw cylindrical shapes for the position of each arm.

Draw in the shape of the lower legs, overlapping them with the thighs where the knee joints would be.

Sketch in the basic shape and direction of the feet.

Draw a teardrop shape for each hand, remembering to think about how the hands would grasp the boulder.

Mark the position of the facial features.

Draw in the basic shape of the figure's torso.

Draw in a large, rugged boulder.

Give your drawing added action by adding small fragments of rock falling off the boulder.

Draw a large shadow under the hero, as the huge boulder casts a shadow too.

Complete the details of the hero's face and torso. Make sure he has a well-defined muscle structure under his costume.

21

Hi-tech spy

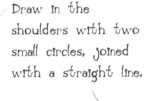

DRAW

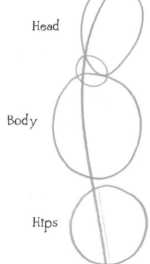

Head

Body

Hips

The hi-tech spy lives in the dangerous and exciting world of espionage. She needs all the latest equipment and technology to stay on top and survive.

Draw in four ellipses, one each for the head, neck, body and hips.

Draw in the shoulders with two small circles, joined with a straight line.

Sketch in the position of the facial features.

Draw in the legs of the spy.

Overlap both sections of each leg to indicate the joints.

Position the earpiece and the glasses.

Draw in the facial features and the hair.

Use straight lines to draw the basic shape of the laptop.

Add in fingers.

Finish the detail to the face and hair.

Complete the details of the head set.

Add a screen image and keyboard to the laptop.

Using long curved lines, add in the spy's coat.

Add clothing details like belt, boots and polo neck top.

Shade areas where light would not reach.

Mutant figure

DRAW

The mutant figure can be anything you can imagine. The figure here is a wolf—man crouching on all fours, ready to attack!

Draw circles for the hips, body, neck and head.

Hips

Neck

Head

Body

Draw two circles for the shoulders and connect them underneath with a straight line.

Sketch overlapping ellipses to create the legs.

Sketch in the position of the feet.

Draw a large circle for each hand.

Each arm is formed with two ellipses, a smaller one overlapping a larger one where they join.

Mutant Heads

These mutant heads will give you some ideas for creating your own mutants!

24

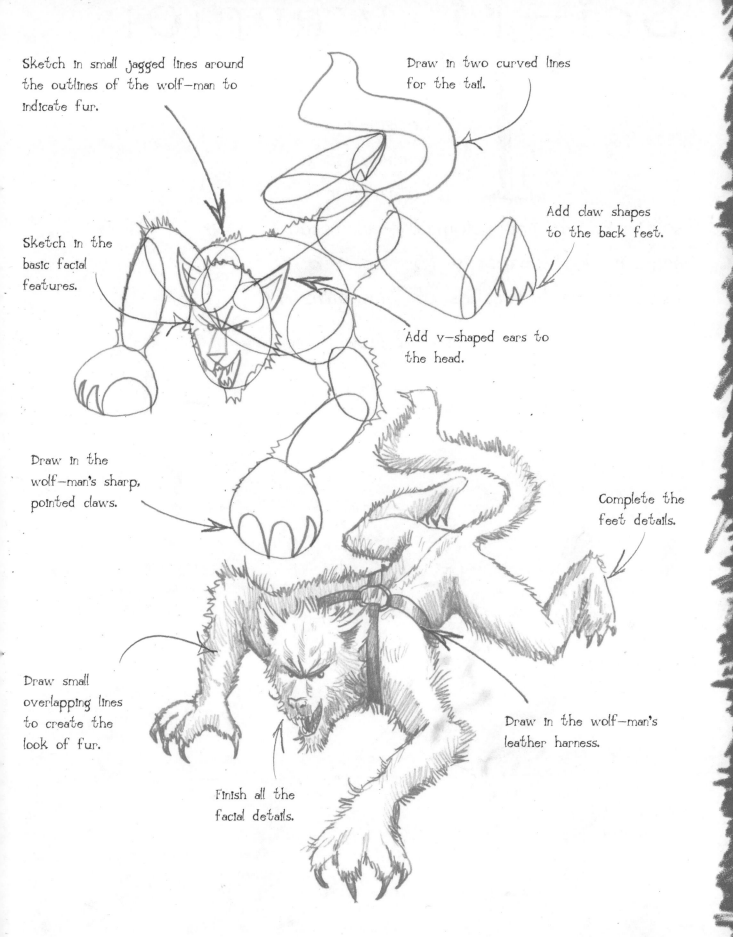

Sketch in small jagged lines around the outlines of the wolf-man to indicate fur.

Draw in two curved lines for the tail.

Sketch in the basic facial features.

Add claw shapes to the back feet.

Add v-shaped ears to the head.

Draw in the wolf-man's sharp, pointed claws.

Complete the feet details.

Draw small overlapping lines to create the look of fur.

Draw in the wolf-man's leather harness.

Finish all the facial details.

25

DRAW Sci-fi warrior

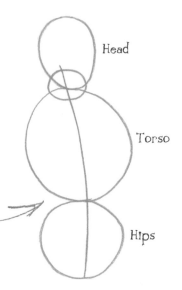

The sci-fi warrior is a futuristic soldier with technologically-advanced armour and weaponry for fighting in the furthest reaches of the galaxy.

Start by drawing four ellipses: one each for the head, neck, torso and hips. Add a curved centre line.

Head

Torso

Hips

Add two small circles on either side of the torso.

Add an oval to each arm for the hands.

Draw a line to position the laser gun.

Sketch in the position of the arms with simple shapes that overlap at the joints.

Add curved lines for the top part of each leg.

Add straight lines for the lower part of each leg.

Draw in the shape and direction of the feet.

Use construction lines as a guide to draw in the basic shape and details of a helmet.

Draw the shape of the laser gun using straight lines.

Roughly sketch in the shape of the fingers.

Add the body armour. Draw lines to indicate the joints in it.

Complete the details of the face and helmet.

Add the jet pack on his back.

Details like this circuit board can give the drawing a more futuristic look.

Draw sharp spiky lines coming out of the end of the gun to create a dramatic effect.

Shade in areas where light would not reach.

Complete the details of the armour. All the shapes should be very precise.

27

Jungle explorer

An expedition into the jungle can be very hazardous so the explorer has to be ready for action. In this drawing the explorer is swinging from a rope.

Head

Torso

Hips

Draw in a centre line for the spine and add three circles for the head, torso and hips.

Draw two circles connected by a line for the shoulders.

Add rounded shapes for the arms that overlap at the shoulder and elbow joints.

Sketch in larger rounded shapes for the thighs.

Draw the lower legs with a simple tube shape, overlapping the top part of the leg to position the knee joints.

Draw two curved lines for the rope.

Draw the basic shape of hands clinging to the rope.

Mark in the position of the facial features.

Use curved lines to create movement in the shape of the hair.

Sketch in the shape of the chest.

Finish the facial details.

Draw lines across the rope to make it look real.

Add a sheathed knife strapped to the belt.

Draw in the character's boots. Show the sole of the boot coming towards you. Remember to use perspective to proportion the boot.

Add the detail of the clothing: top, socks, belt, shorts and pockets.

Add a few movement lines.

29

Cyborg

A cyborg is a combination of man and machine! With its mechanical additions the cyborg is far faster and stronger than a normal human being.

Head

Torso

Hips

Draw in simple shapes for the head, torso and hips with a curved line for the spine. Add a line for the direction of the shoulders.

Sketch in construction lines to give shape and direction to the head.

Draw an oval for the hand.

Extend the direction of the shoulder line forward. Now draw in a long tube using perspective for the outstretched cybernetic arm.

Draw rounded overlapping shapes for the legs.

Add the shape and direction of each foot.

30

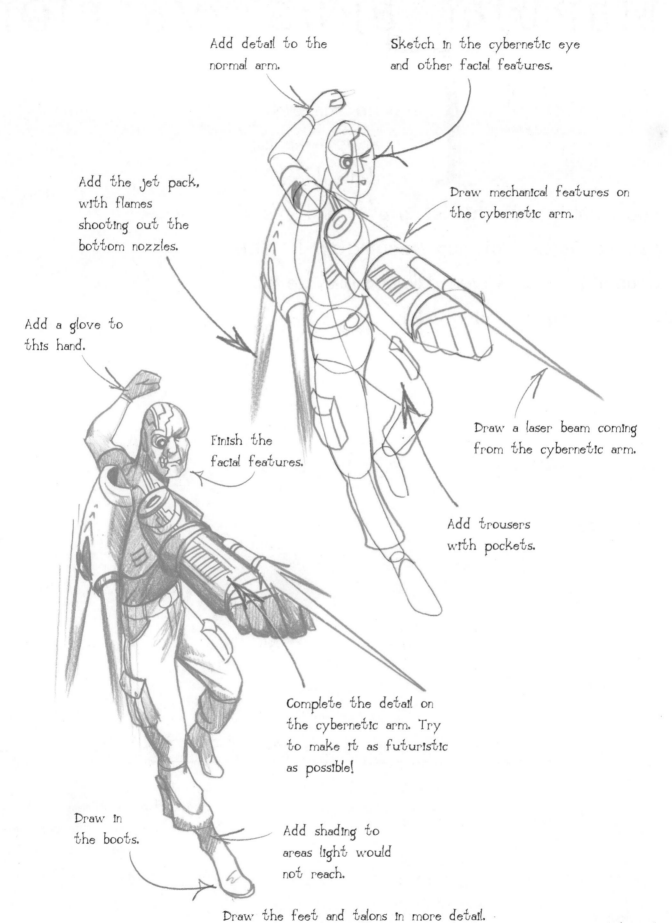

Add detail to the normal arm.

Sketch in the cybernetic eye and other facial features.

Add the jet pack, with flames shooting out the bottom nozzles.

Draw mechanical features on the cybernetic arm.

Add a glove to this hand.

Finish the facial features.

Draw a laser beam coming from the cybernetic arm.

Add trousers with pockets.

Complete the detail on the cybernetic arm. Try to make it as futuristic as possible!

Draw in the boots.

Add shading to areas light would not reach.

Draw the feet and talons in more detail.

Draw Martial Arts Warrior

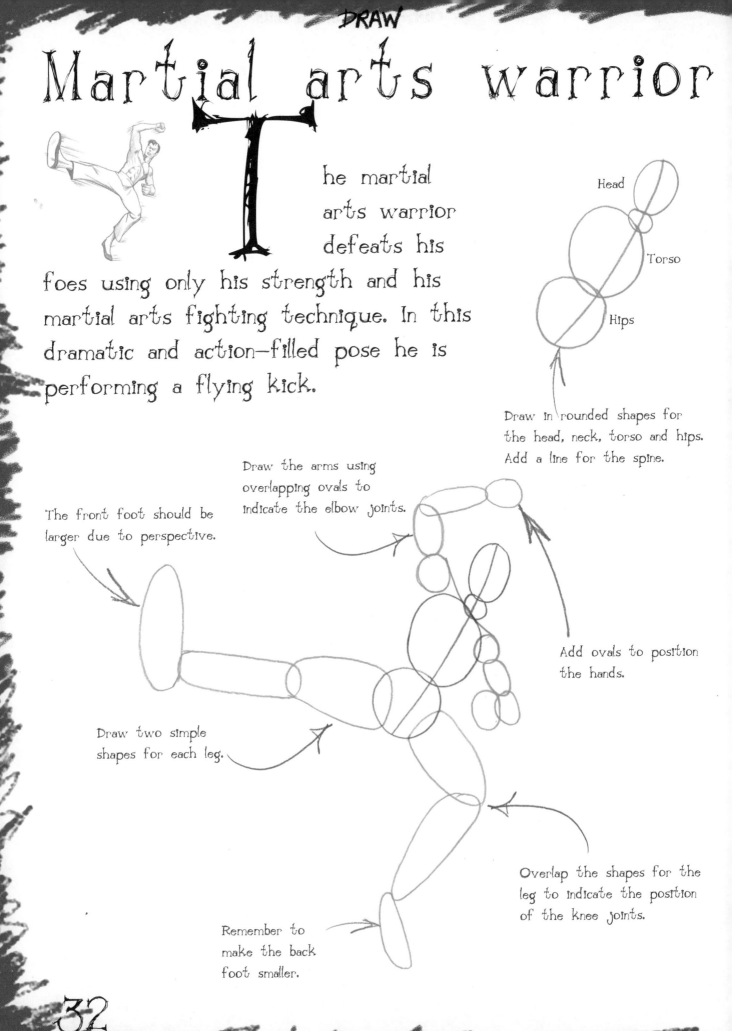

The martial arts warrior defeats his foes using only his strength and his martial arts fighting technique. In this dramatic and action-filled pose he is performing a flying kick.

Head

Torso

Hips

Draw in rounded shapes for the head, neck, torso and hips. Add a line for the spine.

Draw the arms using overlapping ovals to indicate the elbow joints.

The front foot should be larger due to perspective.

Add ovals to position the hands.

Draw two simple shapes for each leg.

Overlap the shapes for the leg to indicate the position of the knee joints.

Remember to make the back foot smaller.

Start to draw in the muscle structure.

Mark the position of the facial features and hair.

Using the construction lines as a guide, draw in both arms and fists.

Draw loose trousers around the legs.

Draw in the shape of the shoes.

Complete the details of the facial features and the hair.

Add tone to define the muscles.

Add muscles to both the arms.

Add lines to indicate the movement of a flying kick.

Draw folds and creases on the trousers.

Add shade to areas where light would not reach.

DRAW
Flying super hero

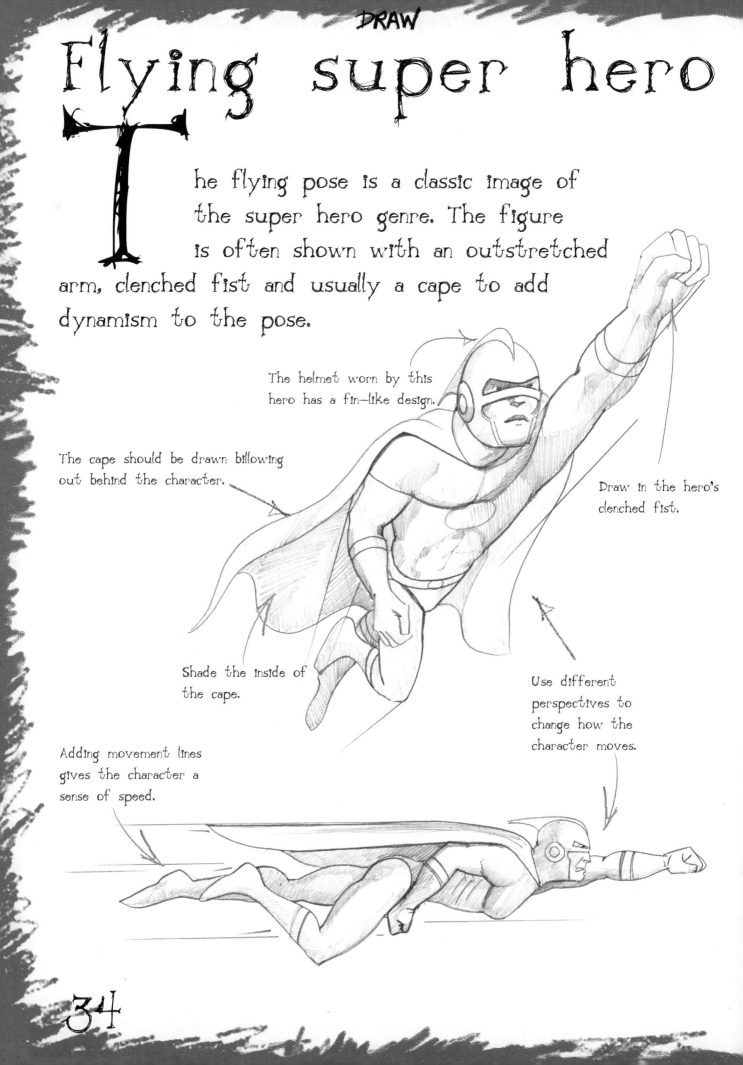

The flying pose is a classic image of the super hero genre. The figure is often shown with an outstretched arm, clenched fist and usually a cape to add dynamism to the pose.

The helmet worn by this hero has a fin—like design.

The cape should be drawn billowing out behind the character.

Draw in the hero's clenched fist.

Shade the inside of the cape.

Use different perspectives to change how the character moves.

Adding movement lines gives the character a sense of speed.

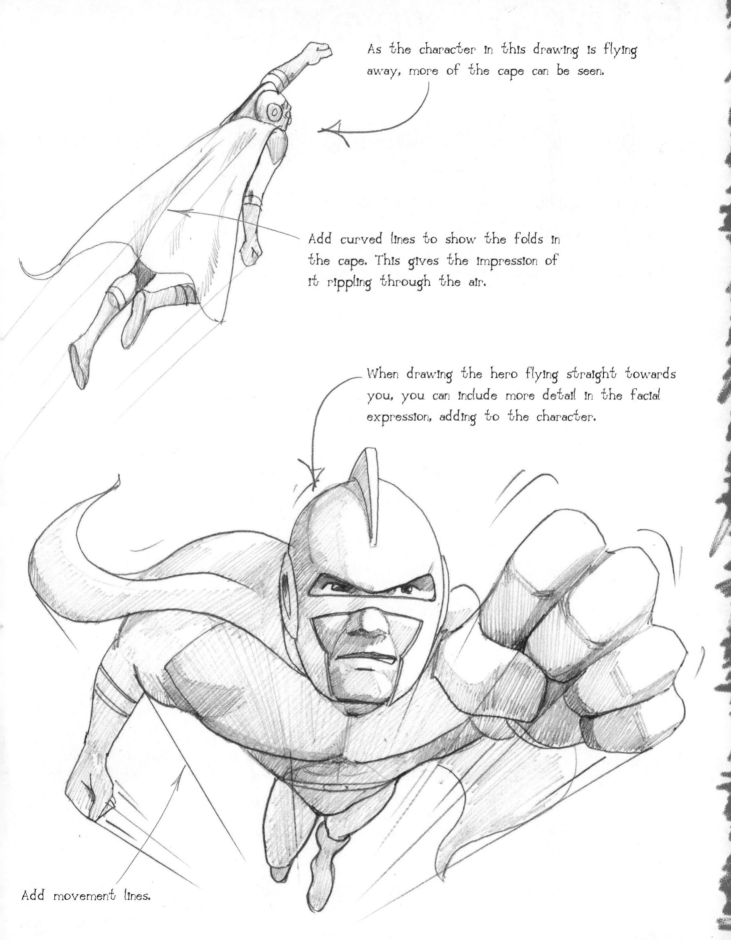

As the character in this drawing is flying away, more of the cape can be seen.

Add curved lines to show the folds in the cape. This gives the impression of it rippling through the air.

When drawing the hero flying straight towards you, you can include more detail in the facial expression, adding to the character.

Add movement lines.

35

Giant mecha

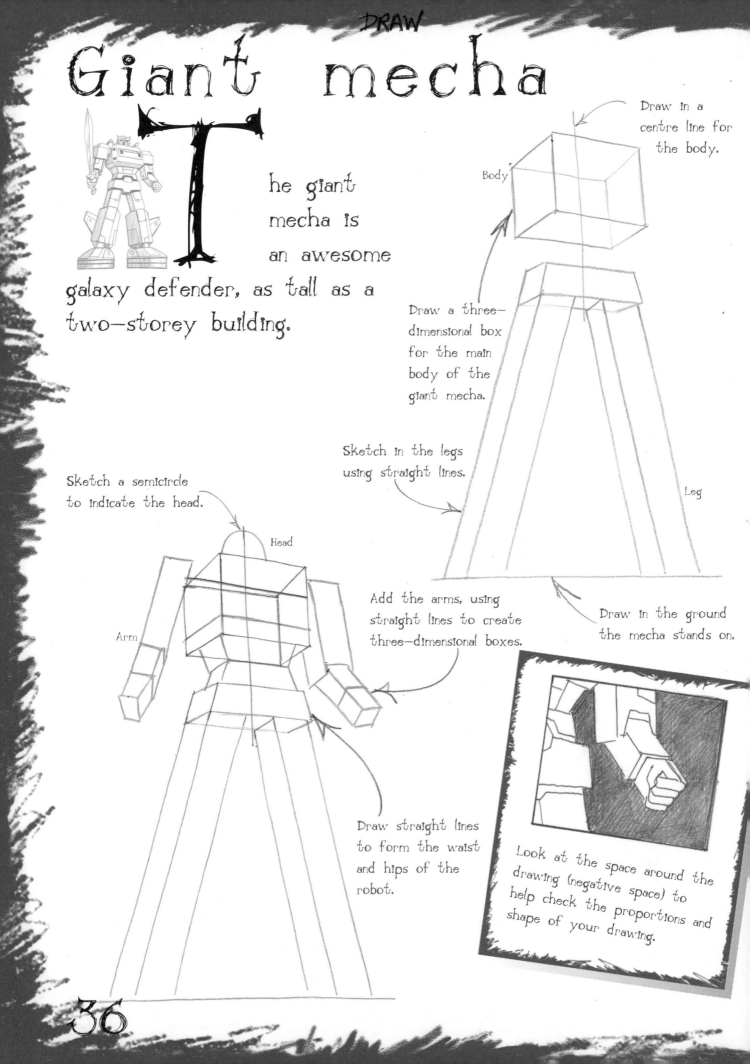

The giant mecha is an awesome galaxy defender, as tall as a two-storey building.

Draw in a centre line for the body.

Body

Draw a three-dimensional box for the main body of the giant mecha.

Sketch in the legs using straight lines.

Leg

Sketch a semicircle to indicate the head.

Head

Arm

Add the arms, using straight lines to create three-dimensional boxes.

Draw in the ground the mecha stands on.

Draw straight lines to form the waist and hips of the robot.

Look at the space around the drawing (negative space) to help check the proportions and shape of your drawing.

Sketch in the sword.

Sketch the details of the face.

Remove your construction lines once you are sure you have finished with them.

Add straight lines to the tops of the arms to form the shoulders.

Using your construction lines as a guide, draw in the hands of the mecha.

Finish the detail of the head.

Shade in one side of the sword.

Draw two large rectangles for the base of the feet, then add the ankle joints and main areas of leg.

Add the detail to the mecha; straight lines on its surface show how it is made mechanically.

Decide on where the light is coming from, then shade the areas where it would not reach.

37

Combat mecha

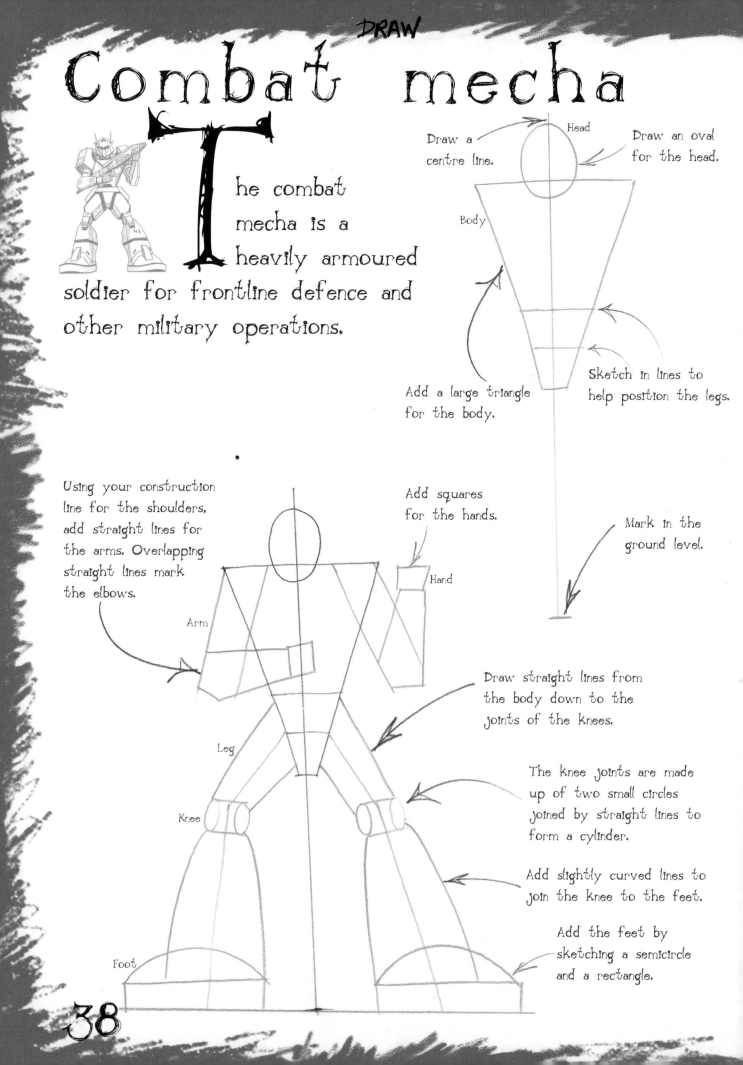

The combat mecha is a heavily armoured soldier for frontline defence and other military operations.

Draw a centre line.

Head

Draw an oval for the head.

Body

Add a large triangle for the body.

Sketch in lines to help position the legs.

Using your construction line for the shoulders, add straight lines for the arms. Overlapping straight lines mark the elbows.

Add squares for the hands.

Hand

Mark in the ground level.

Arm

Draw straight lines from the body down to the joints of the knees.

Leg

The knee joints are made up of two small circles joined by straight lines to form a cylinder.

Knee

Add slightly curved lines to join the knee to the feet.

Add the feet by sketching a semicircle and a rectangle.

Foot

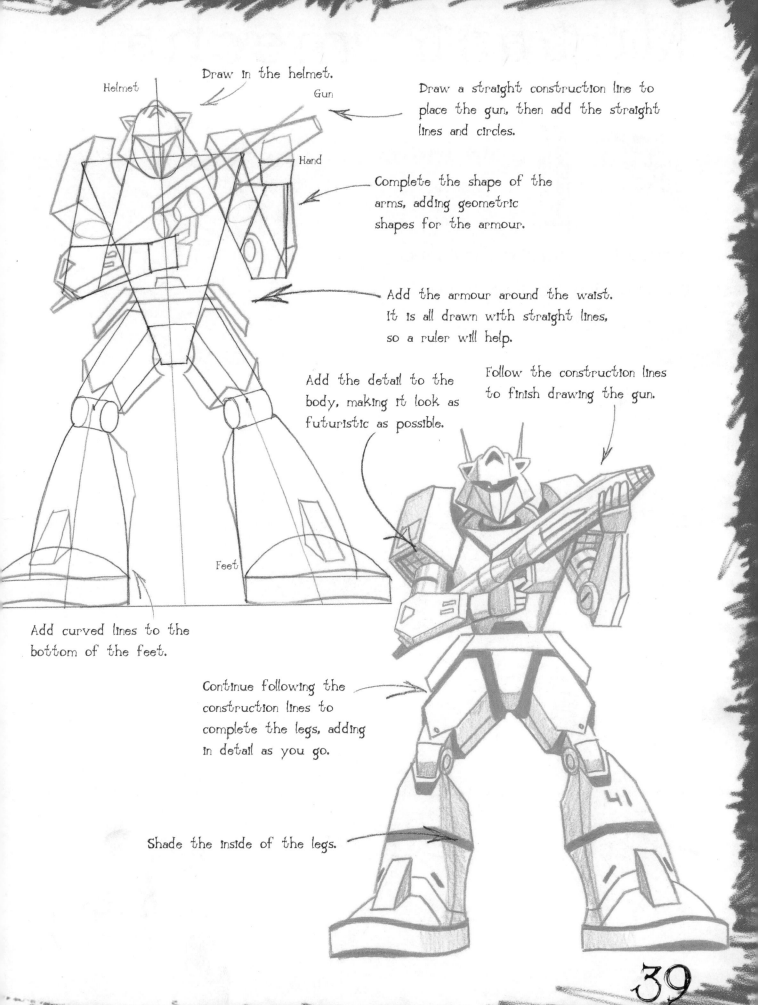

Helmet

Draw in the helmet.

Gun

Draw a straight construction line to place the gun, then add the straight lines and circles.

Hand

Complete the shape of the arms, adding geometric shapes for the armour.

Add the armour around the waist. It is all drawn with straight lines, so a ruler will help.

Add the detail to the body, making it look as futuristic as possible.

Follow the construction lines to finish drawing the gun.

Feet

Add curved lines to the bottom of the feet.

Continue following the construction lines to complete the legs, adding in detail as you go.

Shade the inside of the legs.

39

DRAW Mutant mecha

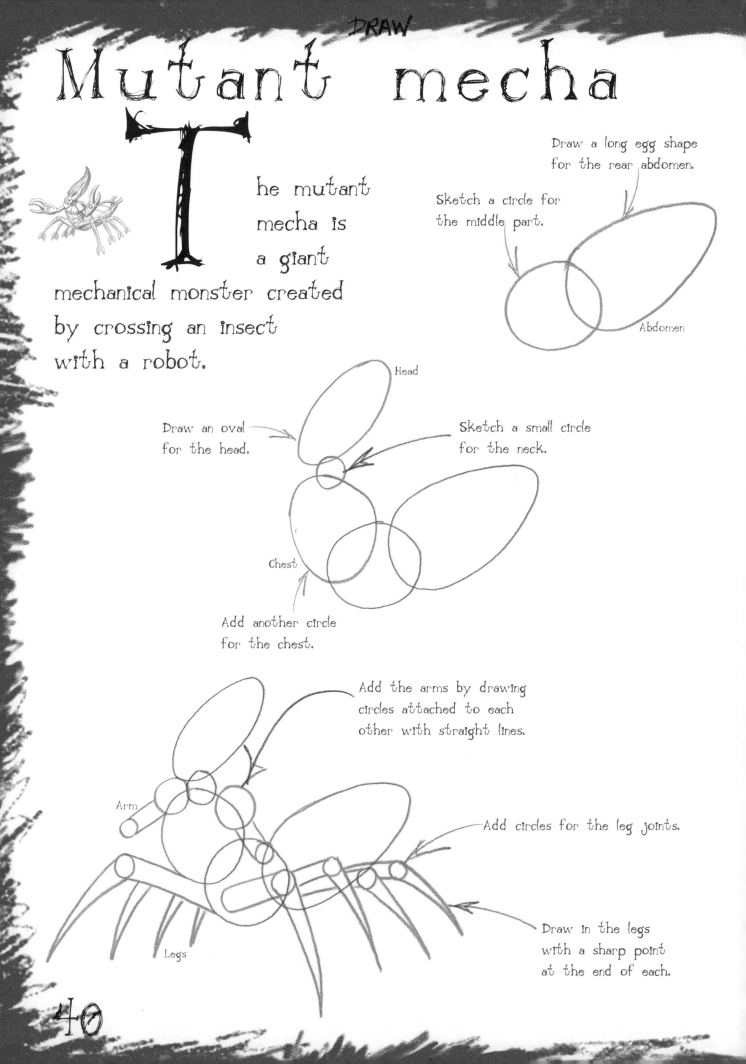

The mutant mecha is a giant mechanical monster created by crossing an insect with a robot.

Draw a long egg shape for the rear abdomen.

Sketch a circle for the middle part.

Abdomen

Head

Draw an oval for the head.

Sketch a small circle for the neck.

Chest

Add another circle for the chest.

Add the arms by drawing circles attached to each other with straight lines.

Arm

Add circles for the leg joints.

Legs

Draw in the legs with a sharp point at the end of each.

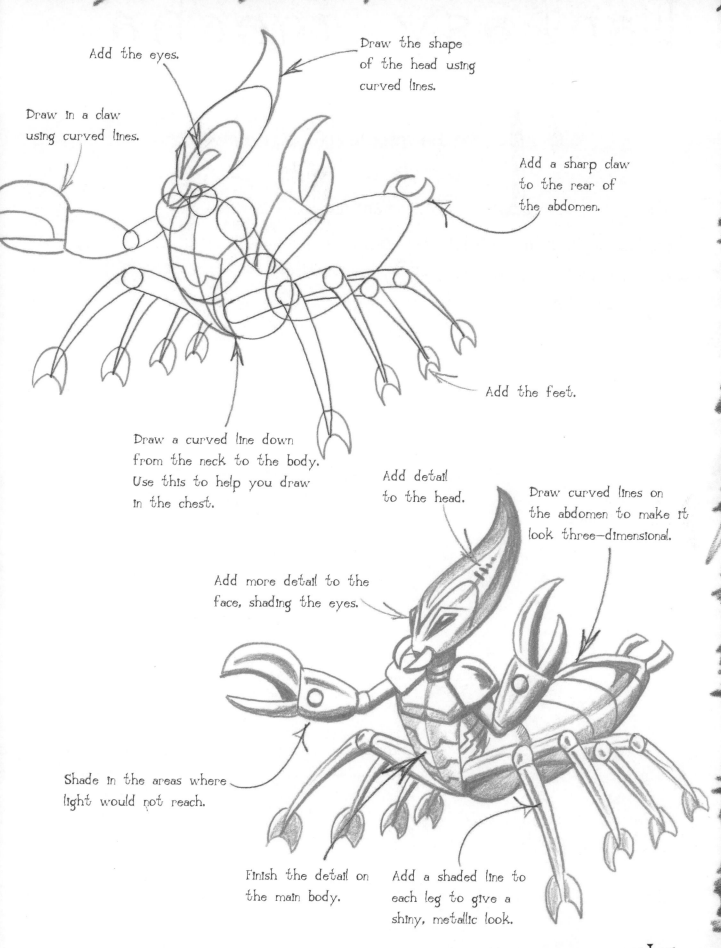

Add the eyes.

Draw the shape of the head using curved lines.

Draw in a claw using curved lines.

Add a sharp claw to the rear of the abdomen.

Add the feet.

Draw a curved line down from the neck to the body. Use this to help you draw in the chest.

Add detail to the head.

Draw curved lines on the abdomen to make it look three-dimensional.

Add more detail to the face, shading the eyes.

Shade in the areas where light would not reach.

Finish the detail on the main body.

Add a shaded line to each leg to give a shiny, metallic look.

DRAW
Fantasy mecha

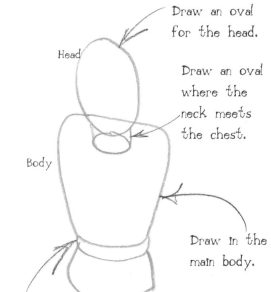

The medieval style of the fantasy mecha takes a knight of old and mixes it with a robot from the future!

Head — Draw an oval for the head.

Draw an oval where the neck meets the chest.

Body — Draw in the main body.

Add a waist.

Draw in the arms, using circles for the joints and hands.

Draw a straight line for the sword.

Draw in the visor using straight lines and curves, making the corners sharp.

Sketch in curves for the shoulder armour.

Arm

Sword

Hand

Sketch in the legs with straight lines.

Add circles for the knees.

Leg

Add circles to the front and side of the knees.

Draw in the lower body armour using curved lines.

Foot

Draw a simple shape for the feet.

Complete the sword with straight lines for the blade and curves for the hilt.

Add the eye slit to the visor.

Add a spike coming from the elbow.

Draw in the armour cuffs with straight lines and curves to make a conical shape.

Draw in the hands using the circular construction lines as guides

Sketch in the cape using long, curved lines.

Cape

Shade areas of the helmet and visor, to give them a metallic look.

Ankle

Add detail to the ankle areas.

Finish the laser sword.

Finish any detail on the armour and remove any unwanted construction lines.

Add detail to the surface of the armour. Small circles can look like bolts holding it together.

Shade where light will not reach.

43

Security DRAW droid

The security droid is small and quick, fitted with useful cameras for all manner of surveillance and defence operations.

Draw a centre line.

Draw a large circle, then two narrow ovals within it to make it look three-dimensional.

Body

Sketch in the construction lines for the shoulder.

Shoulder

Sketch in the legs as straight lines coming down from the shoulders.

Leg

Draw an oval on top of the sphere, then one below it; join these with curved lines.

Sketch more leg detail.

Feet

Add the feet.

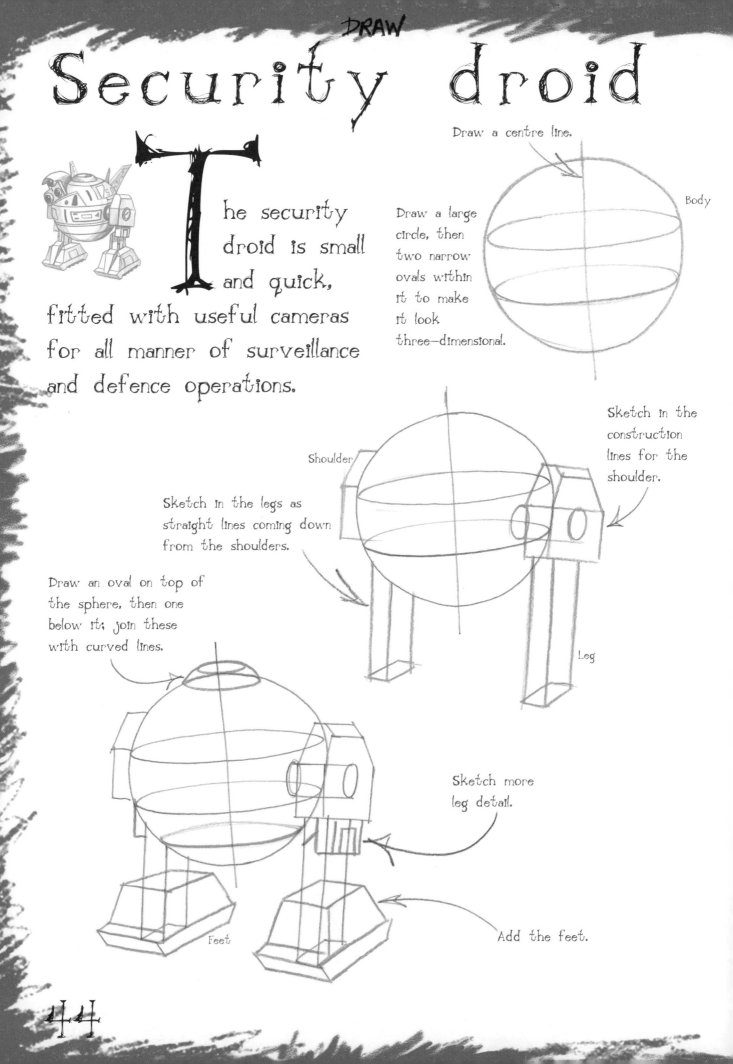

A curved line coming from the top of the robot marks the top of the camera unit.

Draw ovals for the lenses of the camera unit.

Draw rectangles and lines on the body. Remember to curve the lines to keep it looking spherical.

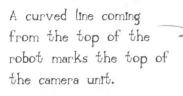
Camera unit

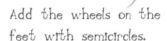
Wheels

The fins on the rear of the bot are drawn with straight lines, forming an almost triangular shape.

Add the wheels on the feet with semicircles.

This detail looks a little like circuit boards. Add some to your drawing to make it look more robotic.

Shade in the lenses of the cameras, adding a highlight to each one for the reflection in the glass.

Shade in the areas where light will not reach.

Complete the detail of the feet.

Complete the shoulders of the security bot.

The straight edges make shading the darkest areas easier.

Drawing a figure

Drawing a cartoon figure can be broken down into stages; follow the steps shown here. By learning how to build up your drawing in this way you can create your own cartoons.

Start by sketching these simple shapes.

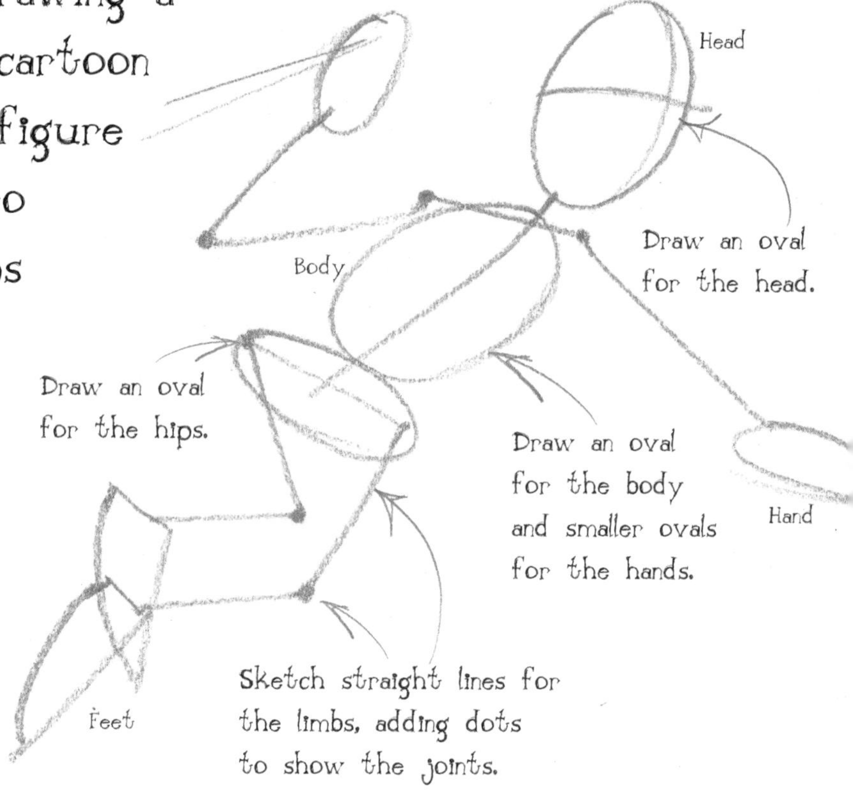

Head

Draw an oval for the head.

Body

Draw an oval for the hips.

Draw an oval for the body and smaller ovals for the hands.

Hand

Sketch straight lines for the limbs, adding dots to show the joints.

Feet

Now start to build up the basic shape and features of your figure.

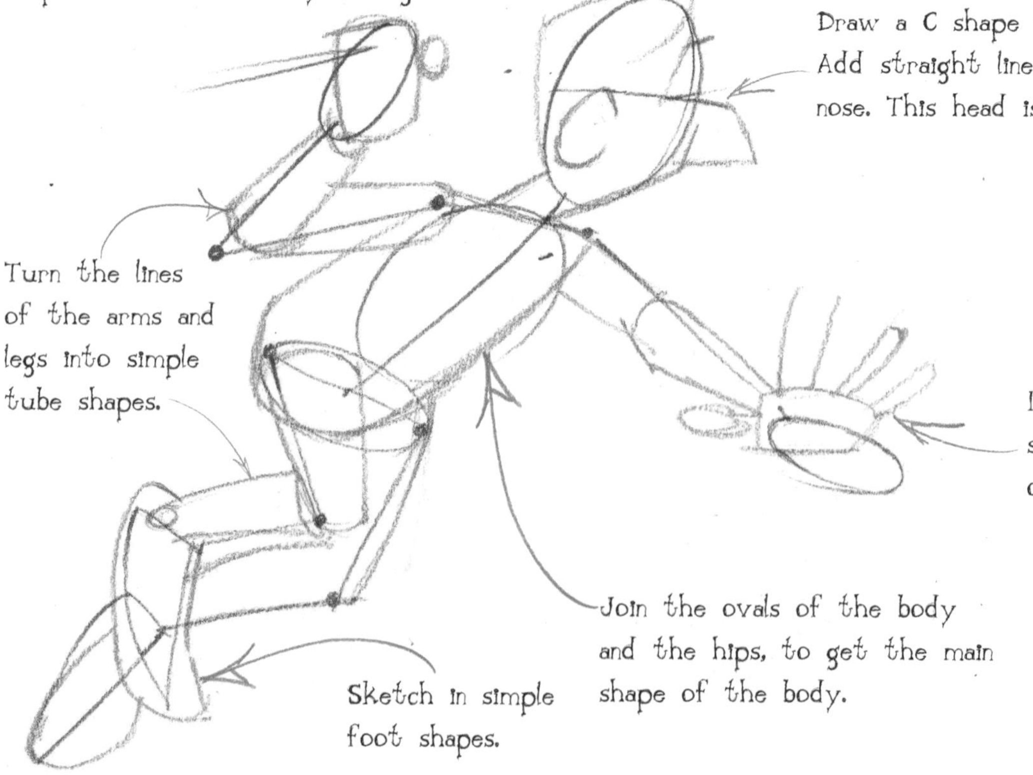

Draw a C shape to position the ear. Add straight lines for the exaggerated nose. This head is in profile (side view).

Turn the lines of the arms and legs into simple tube shapes.

Lightly sketch in the shape of the hand and outstretched fingers.

Sketch in simple foot shapes.

Join the ovals of the body and the hips, to get the main shape of the body.

Now take your figure a stage further.

Add fingers to the clenched fist.

Using a series of simple lines, add details to the head, defining the shape of the nose, eye, ear and hair.

Add the slingshot and satchel.

Draw in the shape of the hand and its fingers.

Draw in the feet and toes.

Draw in the legs. You have already marked where the joints are.

Complete the slingshot, adding detail and shading.

Add shading to the head where necessary, and add lines to show the direction of the hair. Finish off the eyes with a dot for the pupil.

Curved lines like these around an object or figure can suggest movement.

Shade in areas where light wouldn't reach.

Draw in the tunic. Creases in the cloth help to show the direction of the arms and legs beneath.

Use shading on the palm of the hand, and add faint lines to show the joints in the fingers.

Complete any details of the feet and legs, adding toenails and kneecaps.

Carefully rub out any unwanted construction lines that remain.

47

Heads

Heads come in many shapes and sizes, but this simple set of rules should help you draw any type.

First draw an oval (for a longer head and face, just make the oval longer and thinner).

Now add a narrower oval within the first. This is a construction line to show you where the centre line of the face is. The dotted part of this oval represents the back of the head.

Draw a third oval crossing the second one. This is another construction line to help you get the nose and eyes in the right place. Again, the dotted part shows the back of the head.

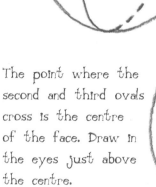

The point where the second and third ovals cross is the centre of the face. Draw in the eyes just above the centre.

With these construction lines in place it is easier to place the facial features and draw the head.

The top of the nose, the middle of the mouth and the space between the eyes should all line up with the second oval.

You can make the head look in a different direction by changing the width of the inner ovals — this changes the position where the lines cross. This is very useful if you want to draw the same head from different angles.

Making the second oval wider makes the head face more to the side. The cross—over construction lines always help you to identify the centre of the face.

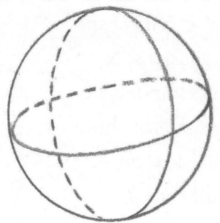

To draw a head facing downwards, the second and third ovals should cross in the lower half of the face. Use the construction lines each time to position the facial features. See how the mouth is mostly hidden by the nose.

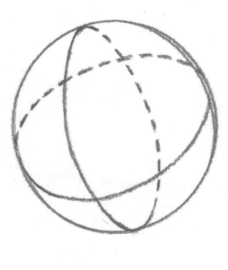

To make the head look upwards, the second and third ovals must cross in the upper half of the face. Again use the construction lines to draw in the features. See how much space the mouth takes up in this view.

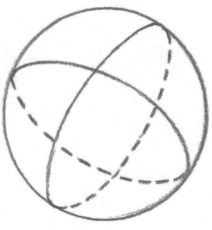

DRAW
Expressions

Drawing different expressions is very important in cartoons. It's the best way to show what your character is thinking or feeling. Try drawing many different facial expressions. Don't be afraid to exaggerate them for comic effect.

Start by drawing an oval shape.

Head

Sketch in the other two ovals as you did before (pages 14—15).

Arched eyebrows.

Angular mouth

Using your construction lines as before, add the basic details of the face. This character looks angry.

Look at your own face in the mirror. By pulling different expressions, you will see how to draw these in your cartoons.

Gritted teeth

Finish the drawing by adding eyes, teeth and hair. Shade in the areas you want to be darker.

Now try drawing some different expressions. Here are a few ideas to get you started.

Giggling

Laughing

Frightened

Tired

Smiling

Puzzled

51

DRAW Characters

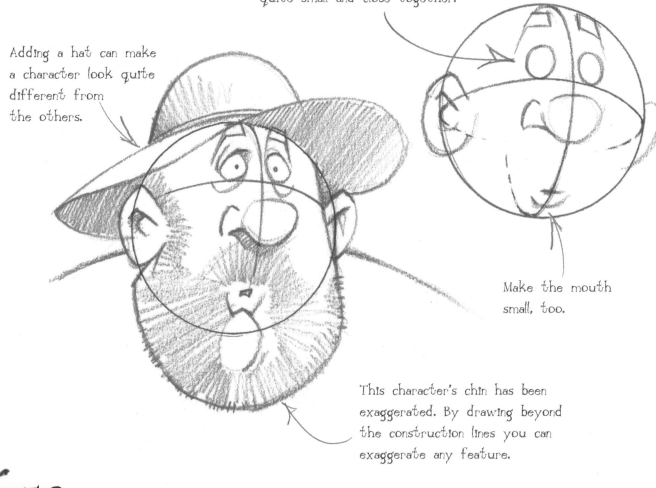

Creating different characters is fun and will expand your cartoon-drawing skills. Try to make each character different from the last. Give each one distinctive features to show their different personalities.

Start by drawing the oval construction lines for a head.

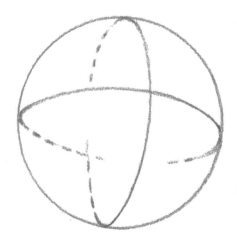

Roughly sketch in the facial features. For this character, draw the eyes quite small and close together.

Adding a hat can make a character look quite different from the others.

Make the mouth small, too.

This character's chin has been exaggerated. By drawing beyond the construction lines you can exaggerate any feature.

Start each character using the oval construction lines for the head.

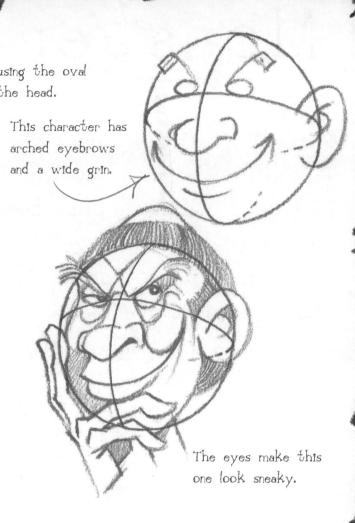

This character's defining features are a long, narrow head, a large nose and a wide mouth.

This character has arched eyebrows and a wide grin.

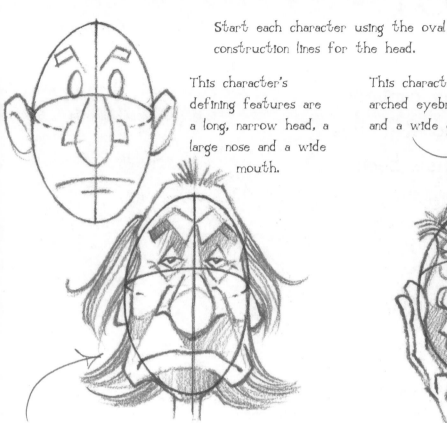

The wide mouth has been exaggerated beyond the construction lines. This makes him look grumpy.

The eyes make this one look sneaky.

This character has high eyebrows, a narrow head and a small mouth, which make him look a bit foolish.

This character's main features are his large, beaklike nose and drooping moustache.

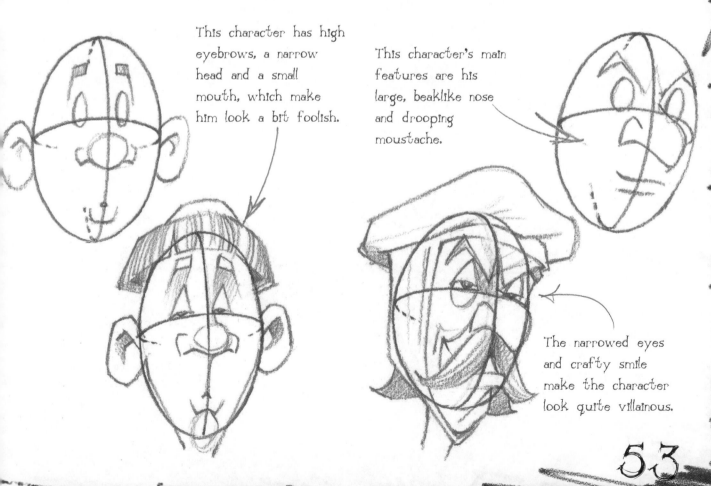

The narrowed eyes and crafty smile make the character look quite villainous.

53

DRAW Monster

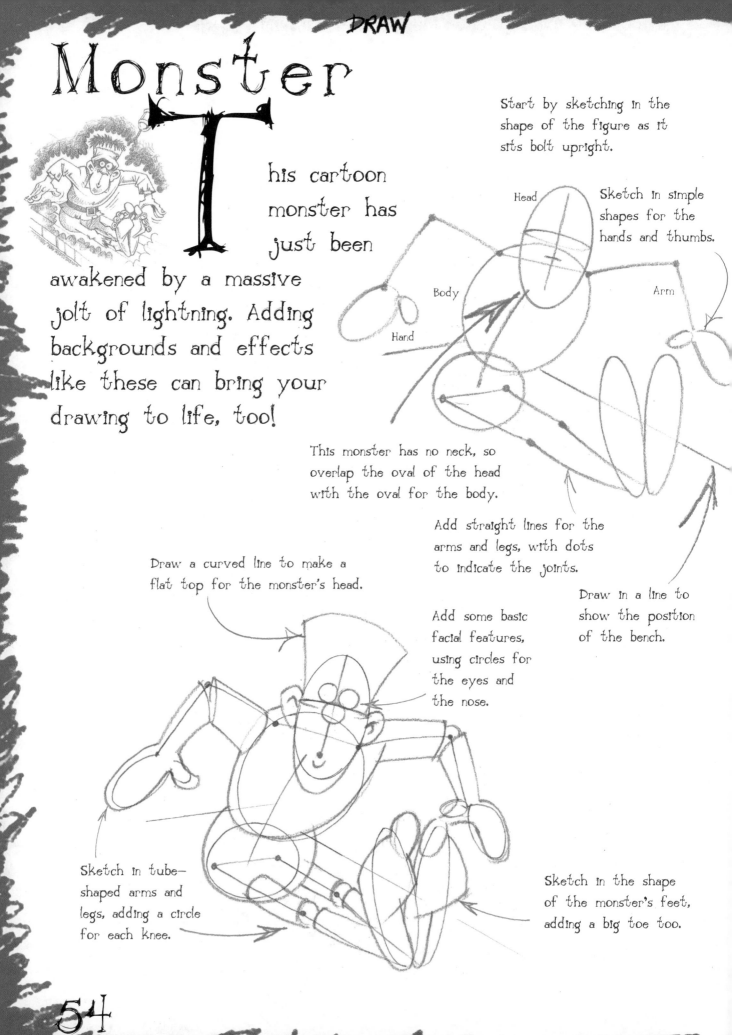

This cartoon monster has just been awakened by a massive jolt of lightning. Adding backgrounds and effects like these can bring your drawing to life, too!

Start by sketching in the shape of the figure as it sits bolt upright.

Sketch in simple shapes for the hands and thumbs.

Head

Body

Arm

Hand

This monster has no neck, so overlap the oval of the head with the oval for the body.

Add straight lines for the arms and legs, with dots to indicate the joints.

Draw in a line to show the position of the bench.

Draw a curved line to make a flat top for the monster's head.

Add some basic facial features, using circles for the eyes and the nose.

Sketch in tube-shaped arms and legs, adding a circle for each knee.

Sketch in the shape of the monster's feet, adding a big toe too.

Sharp, spiky lines coming from the monster show the bolt of electricity.

Add detail to the face. Shading above the eyes makes the brow jut forward.

Draw the monster's sleeves with his arms poking out, to exaggerate his size

Sketch in fingers.

Add the rest of the toes and draw in toenails.

Draw a belt around the monster's waist.

Draw more lines to create the bench.

Finish the detail of the head.

Shading makes the lightning bolt look brighter.

Add stitches to the monster's wrists and forehead.

Finish the details of the hands, adding fingernails and knuckles.

Add shading and creases to the monster's clothes.

Finish drawing the bench.

Remove any unwanted construction lines.

55

Figure work

Adding clothes to a figure can help to define the character. This figure is dressed as a Victorian maid.

Start by sketching these simple shapes for the figure.

Draw an oval for the hand.

Sketch an oval for the head.

Head

Add ovals for the body and hips.

Body

Draw straight lines to connect the ovals and show the positions of the limbs.

Hips

Position the facial features as before.

Inside the hand shape, draw a circle and one finger going into the mouth.

Draw tube shapes for the arms, using your construction lines as a guide.

Indicate the joints with dots.

legs

Join the body and hips into one large oval.

Draw two shapes for the feet.

Feet

Make the legs into tube shapes.

Add a small circle for the position of the big toe. This will help you draw the shoes.

Draw in the position of the big toe.

Drawing hands

1

2

3

4

Follow these steps to help you draw the shape of a hand. As you get better you will be able to draw different hand gestures.

Add more facial features and draw in the shape of the face, using the construction lines as a guide.

Sketch in the hair and add the cap.

Finish the head by adding the hair and eyelashes. Shade above the eyes and inside the ear.

Draw the shape of the clothes going around the body.

Sketch in the dress using curved lines.

Dress

Add details such as cuffs, buttons and a collar.

Add lines to the apron and at the bottom of the dress to show folds in the material.

The hem of the dress covers part of the feet.

Two parallel lines show the soles of the shoes.

Try drawing these hand gestures.

Add shading to areas like this where light wouldn't reach.

Remove any unwanted construction lines.

57

Figure in costume

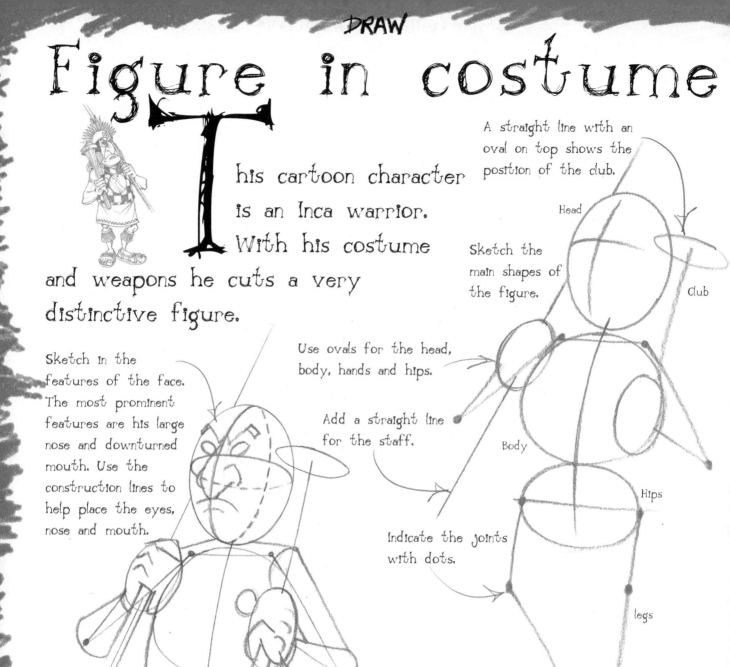

This cartoon character is an Inca warrior. With his costume and weapons he cuts a very distinctive figure.

A straight line with an oval on top shows the position of the club.

Sketch the main shapes of the figure.

Head

Club

Use ovals for the head, body, hands and hips.

Add a straight line for the staff.

Body

Hips

Indicate the joints with dots.

legs

Feet

Sketch in the features of the face. The most prominent features are his large nose and downturned mouth. Use the construction lines to help place the eyes, nose and mouth.

Start to sketch in the shape of the hand.

Draw curved shapes for the position of the feet.

Make the body and hips into one large oval.

Draw in tube-shaped arms and legs. Remember, the dots show where the joints are.

The headdress is made up of diamond shapes. Sketch these along the top of the head.

Extend the shape of the face beyond the construction lines and add more detail to the eyes.

Each of the diamond shapes needs a line down the centre to make it look like a feather.

Sketch in curved lines to draw the club.

Draw in the fingers.

Draw a large circle for the medallion.

Add more detail to the face.

Start sketching in clothes, using simple shapes.

A few wavy lines make the medallion look reflective.

Draw lines down the club to give it a wood effect.

Shade areas like this where light wouldn't reach.

Add toes and sandals to the feet.

Shade alternate squares on the warrior's tunic.

Add lines to show costume detail.

Complete the details of the feet and sandals.

Remove any unwanted construction lines.

59

Man on a donkey

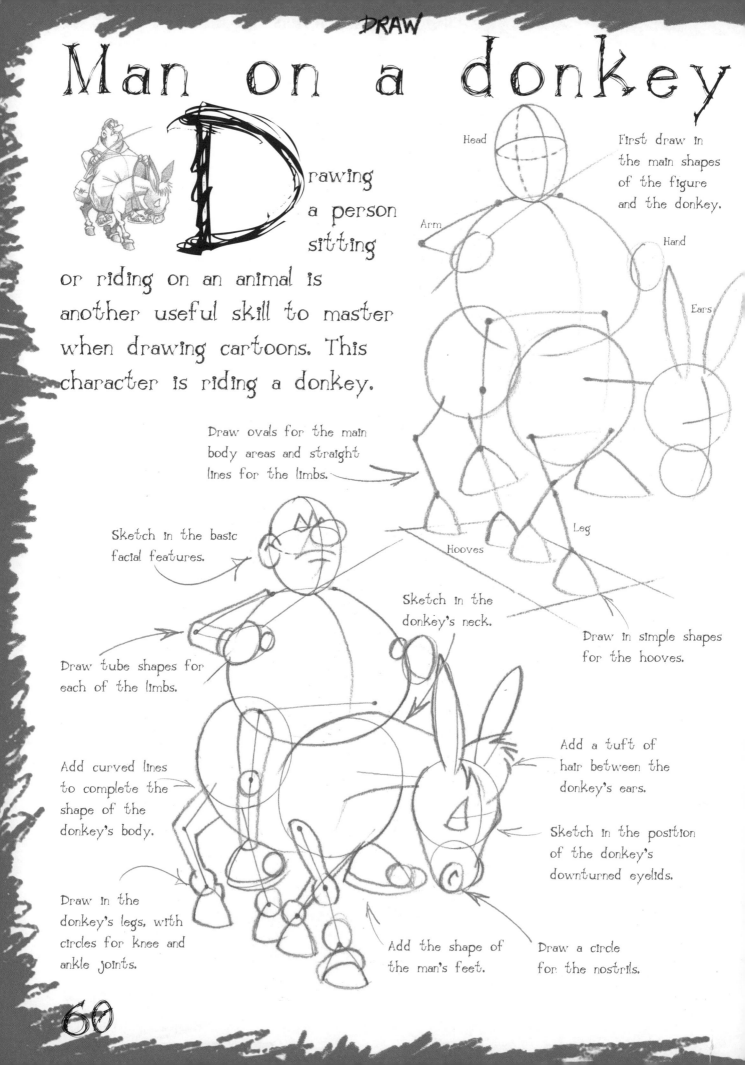

Drawing a person sitting or riding on an animal is another useful skill to master when drawing cartoons. This character is riding a donkey.

First draw in the main shapes of the figure and the donkey.

Head

Arm

Hand

Ears

Draw ovals for the main body areas and straight lines for the limbs.

Sketch in the basic facial features.

Sketch in the donkey's neck.

Leg

Hooves

Draw in simple shapes for the hooves.

Draw tube shapes for each of the limbs.

Add curved lines to complete the shape of the donkey's body.

Add a tuft of hair between the donkey's ears.

Sketch in the position of the donkey's downturned eyelids.

Draw in the donkey's legs, with circles for knee and ankle joints.

Add the shape of the man's feet.

Draw a circle for the nostrils.

Add clothes to the man.

Add hair and more facial features.

Sketch in fingers.

Add lines to show the inside of the donkey's ears.

Draw in the reins and bridle.

Finish the detail on the head, shading under the chin and around the neck.

Complete the detail of the hands.

Shade the back of the donkey's ear.

Draw the shape of the donkey's legs in more detail.

Add toes to the man's feet.

Add lines for creases in the robe's material.

Framing your drawing with a square or rectangle can make it look completely different.

Shade areas where light would not reach.

Add final details to the man's feet and to the donkey's hooves.

Remove any unwanted construction lines.

DRAW Cartoon aliens

There are no rules when drawing aliens. Add extra eyes and legs, draw hands with three fingers or draw the neck very long and skinny. Perhaps even add a flying saucer!

To make this one-eyed alien, start by drawing two ovals joined by a long tube shape.

Add two rounded shapes for feet.

Draw curved lines for arm shapes.

Add shading to the areas where light would not reach.

Draw in markings on the alien's body.

Add one large eye and shading.

Add details to the feet.

Here is a cute alien with his own flying saucer.

To start with draw two basic ovals and a semi-circle.

Mark in the mouth.

Add five small ovals for the alien's eyes.

Draw more oval shapes at the arms and neck.

Sketch in two alien antennae.

Mark in the eyes.

Draw in small rounded shapes on the bottom of the flying saucer.

Add ear shapes to the side of the head.

Draw in the detail on the face.

Draw curved shapes for two arms.

Shade in the areas where light would not reach.

Draw in the fuel tank on the front of the saucer.

Add the exhaust underneath the flying saucer.

Remove any unwanted construction lines.

DRAW Spaceman and robots

This spaceman loves to explore new planets, especially when he stumbles across new and interesting alien robots!

Draw two large circles slightly overlapping.

Draw in a visor shape on the helmet.

Sketch in two curved arm shapes.

Shade in the visor, leave a spot white for a highlight.

Add detail to the face of the space man.

Draw in curved leg shapes.

Draw in fingers.

Add basic rounded shapes for the feet.

Indicate the shape of an oxygen pack.

Add shading and detail to the space suit.

Draw vertical lines on the base of the space boots.

Start by drawing basic rounded shapes for the outlines of the two robots.

You can use different-sized shapes to create different characters.

Add circles to mark the positions of the arms.

Add an antenna.

Add rounded shapes with circle knee joints.

Draw eyes and a mouth.

Shade the robots to look like shiny metal.

Draw in rounded foot shapes.

Add branch shapes for arms.

Add the arms using straight lines and circle shapes.

Shade the areas where light would not reach.

65

Pirate trio

This character doesn't look too happy. Has he been taken prisoner or are his mates giving him a helping hand? This pose captures the sense of weight that the other two are supporting.

Sketch in ovals for the heads, bodies and hips.

Use straight lines to position the arms and legs with dots for joints.

Indicate the direction of each head by sketching the position of the facial features.

Add simple shapes for the hands and feet.

Draw in ovals for the knees.

Draw in tube shapes for the arms and legs.

Sketch in the
pirate's headwear.

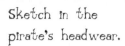

Draw in the ears and facial features.

Start to draw in the
main shapes of the
clothing and shoes.

Finish off all details to
the clothes and heads.

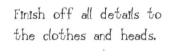

Add detail to
areas of the
costume, such as
stripy socks.

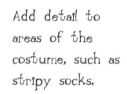

The sagging tunic adds weight
to the body.

Shade in areas where light wouldn't reach.

Pirates in action

Pirates relied on speed and terror to attack their victim's ship. Once on board they fought with great fury. This action pose captures the cut and thrust of the attack.

Draw ovals for the head, body and hips of both figures.

Sketch in the straight lines for the arms and legs with dots for joints.

Sketch straight lines for the weapons.

Add simple shapes for the hands and feet.

Note the angle of the feet.

Position the eyes, nose and ears.

Using the construction lines as a guide, draw in the main shapes of the bodies.

Draw in the tube shapes for the arms and legs.

Add fingers and thumbs to the hands.

Add details to the weapons.

Draw in the hat shapes curving around the head.

Sketch large cuffs on the coat.

Add tall over-the-knee boots.

Draw in boots with a fold over the top.

Add detail to the faces and hair.

Draw in all the finishing details to the clothing and boots.

Finish off the daggers and swords.

Add shading to the areas that light wouldn't reach.

Add detail to the faces and hair.

Add buckles.

Remove any unwanted construction lines.

69

Draw Dracula's castle

Dracula's castle sits atop a craggy mountain, ominous and scary.

Start by using two-point perspective to draw the basic shapes of all the towers.

Draw construction lines for the top parts of the towers.

Adding shade

In order to give your drawing a feeling of solidity, first decide what direction the light is coming from. Then shade areas where the light wouldn't reach. Use a light tone for areas that get a little light.

Start to add the mountain and the bridge.

Sketch in the basic structure for each of the windows.

Add structural design details to the towers.

Add the window frames.

Begin to add shade to the sides of the castle not getting much light.

Draw in the roof tiles.

Add long lines curving down from the castle for the buttresses (wall supports).

Add a moon and some creepy bat silhouettes.

Add dark shading for the windows.

Add shade to the side of the building.

Draw lines for the texture of the mountain.

Remove any unwanted construction lines.

71

Pirate skull castle

Pirates live in this spooky castle made from a giant skull and bones. They shoot cannons at their enemies from the eyes and mouth.

Start by drawing a circle for the skull.

Sketch two large bone shapes behind the skull.

Add some curved lines to the tops of the bones.

Draw three rounded shapes for the eyes and nose.

Shade in the hollows of the eyes.

Sketch straight lines to create cheekbones.

Add doorways and sketch curved lines for staircases.

Position the mouth and shade it in.

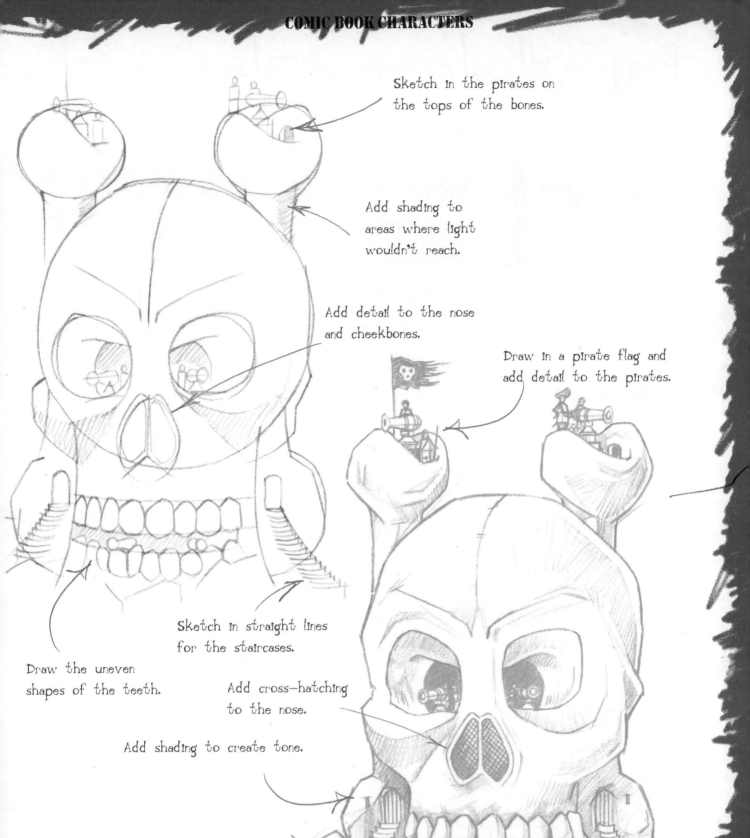

Sketch in the pirates on the tops of the bones.

Add shading to areas where light wouldn't reach.

Add detail to the nose and cheekbones.

Draw in a pirate flag and add detail to the pirates.

Sketch in straight lines for the staircases.

Draw the uneven shapes of the teeth.

Add cross-hatching to the nose.

Add shading to create tone.

Finish off the detail on the staircases and doorways.

Add a rocky texture on the ground.

Remove any unwanted construction lines.

DRAW Fairytale castle

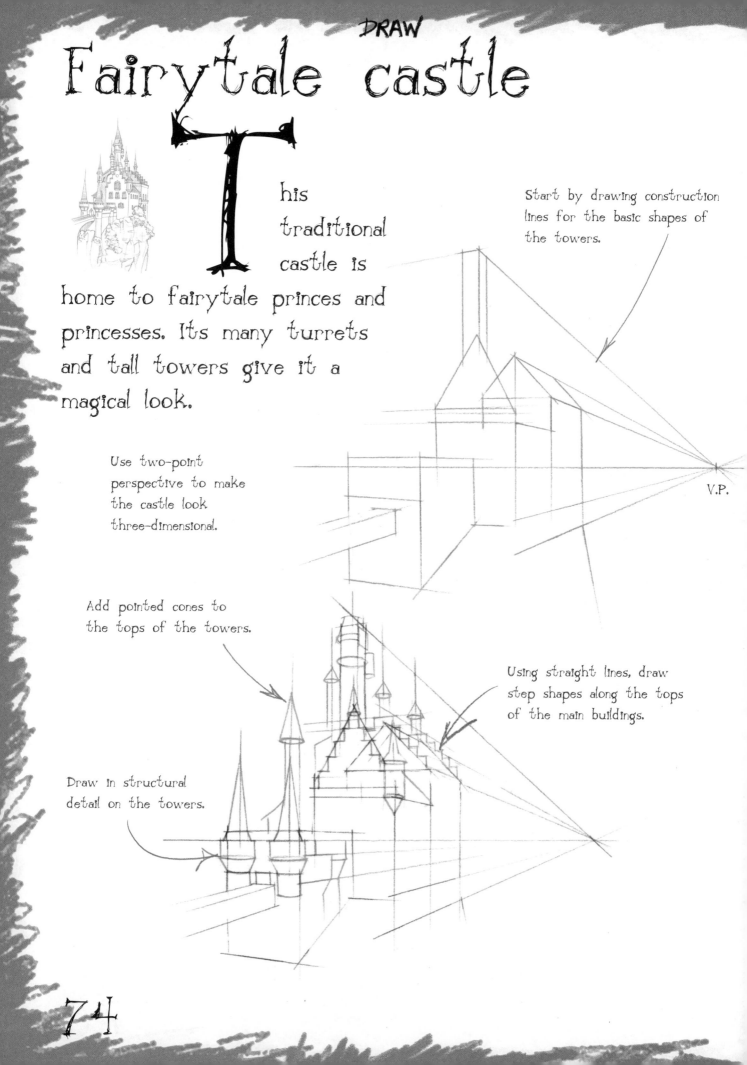

This traditional castle is home to fairytale princes and princesses. Its many turrets and tall towers give it a magical look.

Use two-point perspective to make the castle look three-dimensional.

Start by drawing construction lines for the basic shapes of the towers.

V.P.

Add pointed cones to the tops of the towers.

Using straight lines, draw step shapes along the tops of the main buildings.

Draw in structural detail on the towers.

Add detail to the castle towers.

Mark in the positions of the windows.

Add battlements.

Use horizontal lines to create the tiled tops of the towers.

Draw in the arched detail of the windows.

Shade in areas where light would not reach.

Draw bushes using lots of little lines.

Shade the towers to look three-dimensional.

Shade the base of the castle to look like rock.

Remove any unwanted construction lines.

75

Creating character

DRAW

Creating a scary character can be a great deal of fun. Different characters and features can all be created from the same basic starting point.

Basic Head Construction.

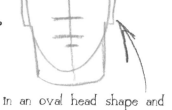

Draw in an oval head shape and mark in the position of facial features with construction lines.

Frankenstein's monster

Vampire

Devil

Grim Reaper

Zombie

Witch

Vampiress

Ghost

Try to see how many different characters you can create from your imagination.

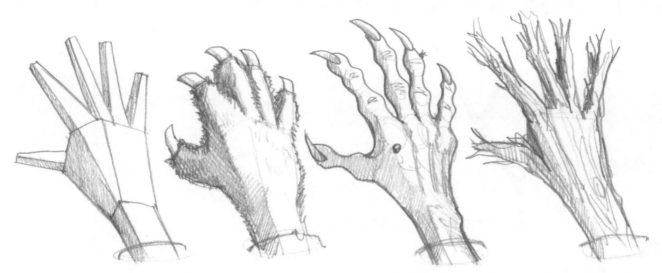

Draw in a basic hand shape with straight construction lines.

Here are a few examples of how scary monster hands can be created from the first template.

Accessories:

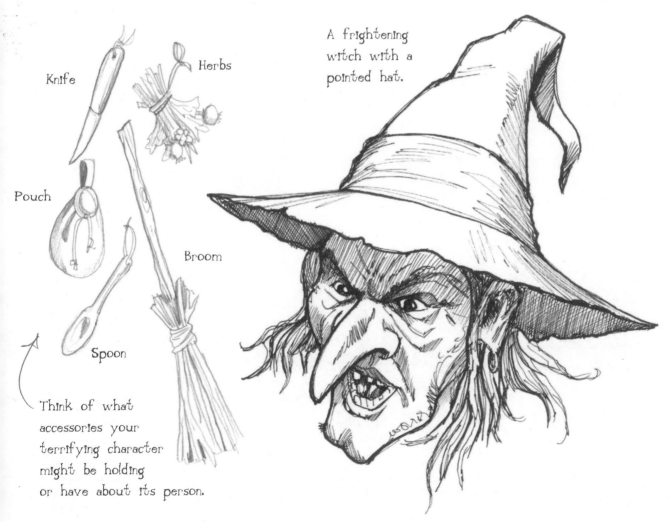

Knife

Herbs

A frightening witch with a pointed hat.

Pouch

Broom

Spoon

Think of what accessories your terrifying character might be holding or have about its person.

Drawing movement

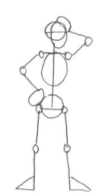

You can make your drawing much more dynamic by giving it a sense of movement.

Start by drawing stick figures in action poses.

These can be the basis of your drawing showing where each limb is according to the position of the body.

A jumping ghoul

This ghoul is mid-jump. You can see how this pose is developed from the stick figure shown.

This finished drawing gives a sense of action. Adding movement lines around the drawing gives it a sense of momentum. The horse's mane and tail also fly out behind it as do the billowing clothes of the grim reaper.

Zombie

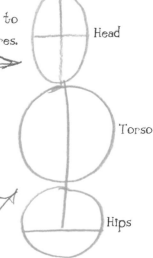

The 'dead' have risen and are walking the earth! The zombies will not stop until they have killed you and made you one of their own.

Sketch in basic construction lines to place facial features.

Head

Torso

Hips

Draw an oval for the head and two circles for the torso and hips. Join these with a centre line.

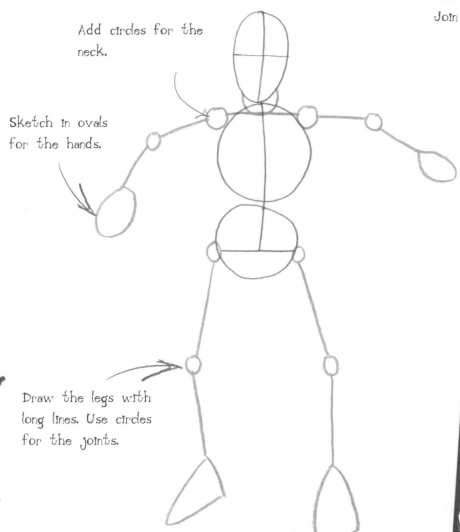

Add circles for the neck.

Sketch in ovals for the hands.

Draw the legs with long lines. Use circles for the joints.

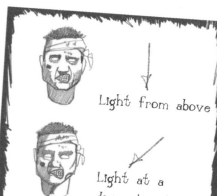

Light from above

Light at a diagonal angle from above.

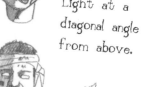

Light from the side

Light from below

Changing the direction of the light source in a drawing can create drama and mood.

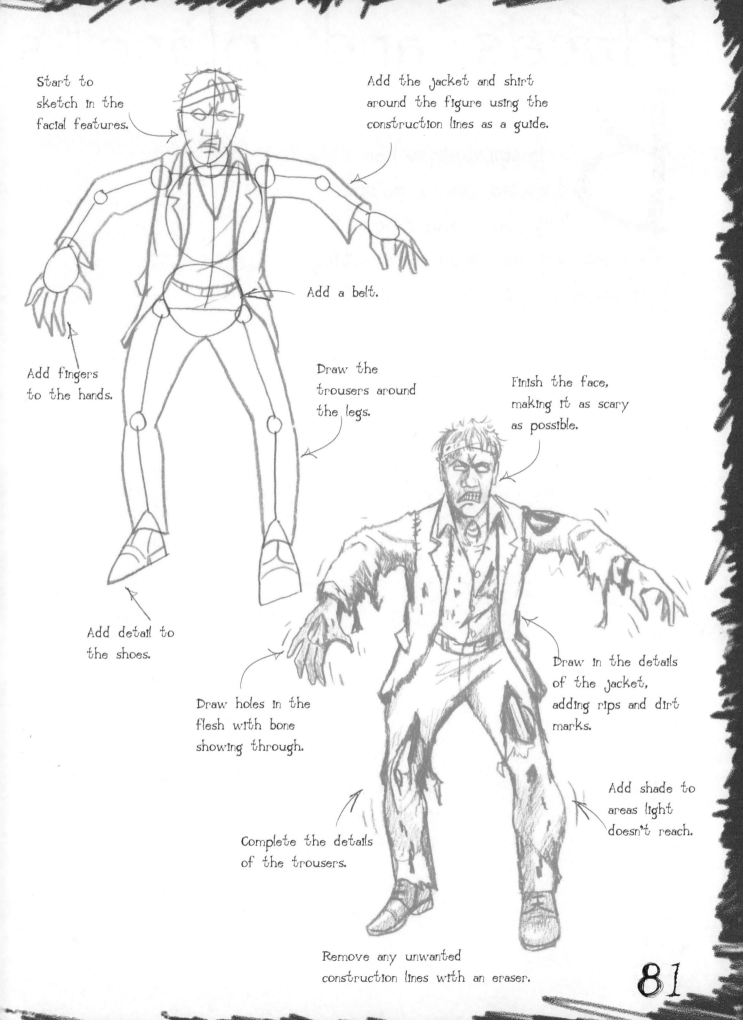

Start to sketch in the facial features.

Add the jacket and shirt around the figure using the construction lines as a guide.

Add a belt.

Add fingers to the hands.

Draw the trousers around the legs.

Finish the face, making it as scary as possible.

Add detail to the shoes.

Draw holes in the flesh with bone showing through.

Draw in the details of the jacket, adding rips and dirt marks.

Add shade to areas light doesn't reach.

Complete the details of the trousers.

Remove any unwanted construction lines with an eraser.

81

Places and planets

Be imaginative when drawing places in space. Try to make the landscapes and settings as exciting or unusual as possible.

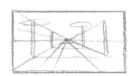

Roughly sketch construction lines for your drawings to help you.

Experiment by changing the eye level and vanishing points of your drawings (see page 8) to create a sense of drama.

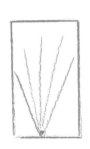

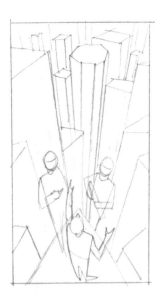
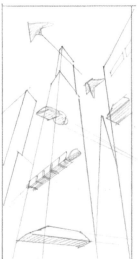

Once you have the basic shape of the drawing you can start to add windows and other final details.

Use hatching to create
the texture of rock.

Draw stars and planets in the sky.

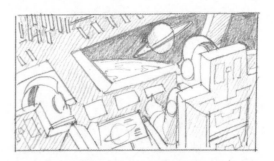

Try to draw something
interesting in both the
foreground and background.

To make your drawing look three—dimensional,
decide which side the light is coming from
so you can put in areas of shadow.

Draw Spacecraft

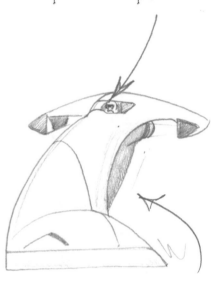

Space travellers use all sorts of unusual flying machines to move around space. Just like cars and planes today, they come in many different shapes and sizes.

Add a space traveller inside the cockpit of the spacecraft.

Start by drawing the basic shapes.

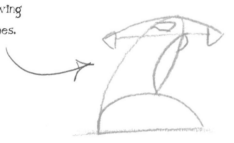

Draw two oval shapes joined together by a smaller rectangle.

Shade areas to make it appear three-dimensional.

Use bold, sweeping curves to the shapes to make it look futuristic.

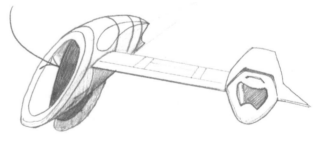

Use perspective (see pages 8—9) to make the craft look as though it is hurtling through space.

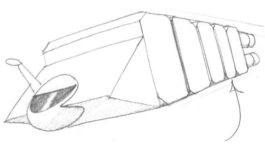

Round off the corners of the shapes.

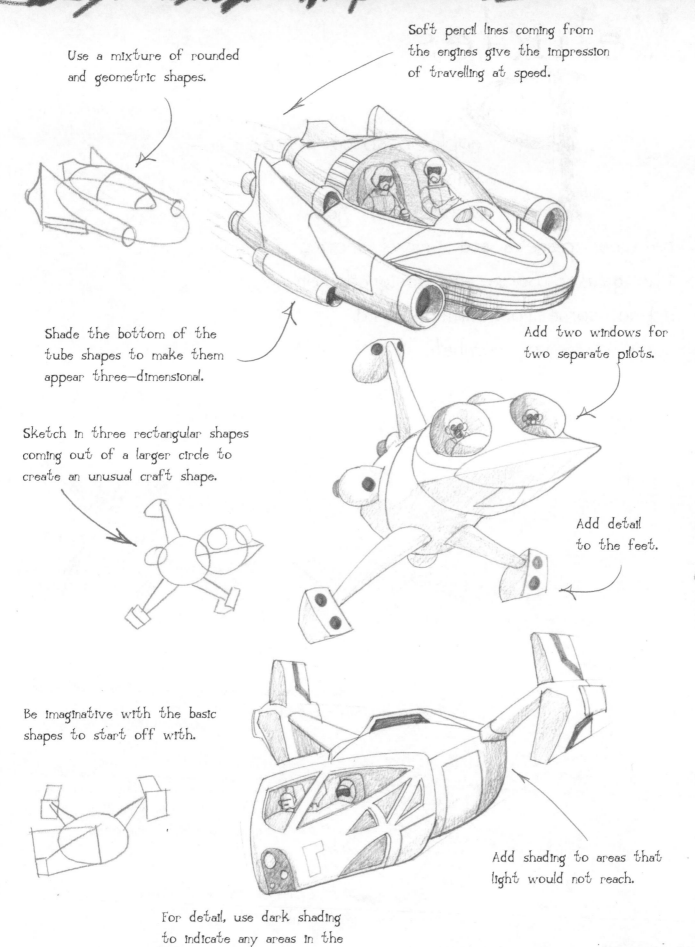

Use a mixture of rounded and geometric shapes.

Soft pencil lines coming from the engines give the impression of travelling at speed.

Shade the bottom of the tube shapes to make them appear three-dimensional.

Add two windows for two separate pilots.

Sketch in three rectangular shapes coming out of a larger circle to create an unusual craft shape.

Add detail to the feet.

Be imaginative with the basic shapes to start off with.

Add shading to areas that light would not reach.

For detail, use dark shading to indicate any areas in the bodywork that go inward.

85

Vehicles

People in space drive various types of vehicles to jet between planets and travel around the galaxy. Some are designed for speed, some for comfort and some even for combat.

For this space scooter, start by sketching a large oval shape with a triangle at the front.

Add curved lines and rounded shapes for the detail of the vehicle.

Draw an oval for the head, with helmet detail.

Add tube shapes for limbs.

Shade the front of the vehicle to look like glass.

Sketch triangle shapes on the front of the machine.

Draw circles for the joints.

Complete the detail of the driver by shading in the helmet and making his suit look futuristic.

Shade in the areas where light would not reach.

Remove any unwanted construction lines.

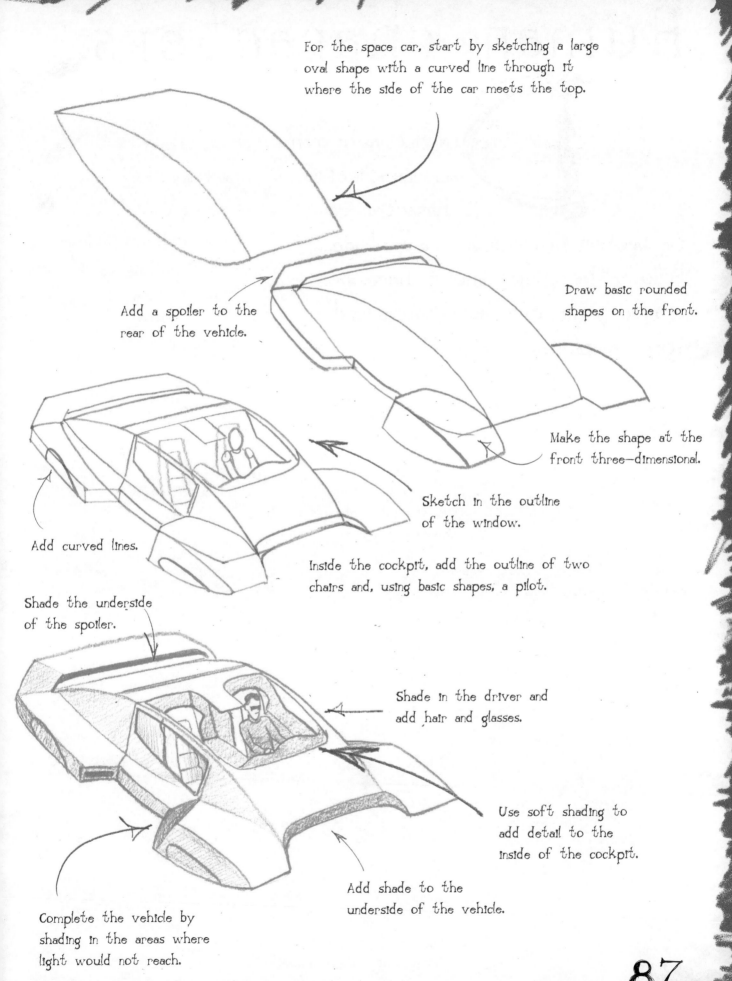

For the space car, start by sketching a large oval shape with a curved line through it where the side of the car meets the top.

Draw basic rounded shapes on the front.

Add a spoiler to the rear of the vehicle.

Make the shape at the front three-dimensional.

Sketch in the outline of the window.

Add curved lines.

Inside the cockpit, add the outline of two chairs and, using basic shapes, a pilot.

Shade the underside of the spoiler.

Shade in the driver and add hair and glasses.

Use soft shading to add detail to the inside of the cockpit.

Add shade to the underside of the vehicle.

Complete the vehicle by shading in the areas where light would not reach.

87

Human characters
DRAW

Drawing a human science-fiction character can be broken down into easy stages. Follow the steps shown here to create your own astronauts and space explorers.

Start by sketching these simple shapes.

Draw circle and oval shapes for the head, main body and hips.

Add hair.

Use straight guidelines and a vertical centre line to experiment with the proportions of the body.

Draw straight lines for the limbs and circles for the joints.

Then, start to build up the basic shapes and features of the figure.

Change the stance of the figure by moving the straight lines of the limbs.

Turn the lines of the arms and legs into simple tube shapes.

Use construction lines to position the features of the face.

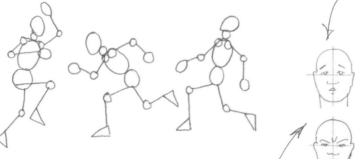

Don't be afraid to exaggerate the features for comic effect.

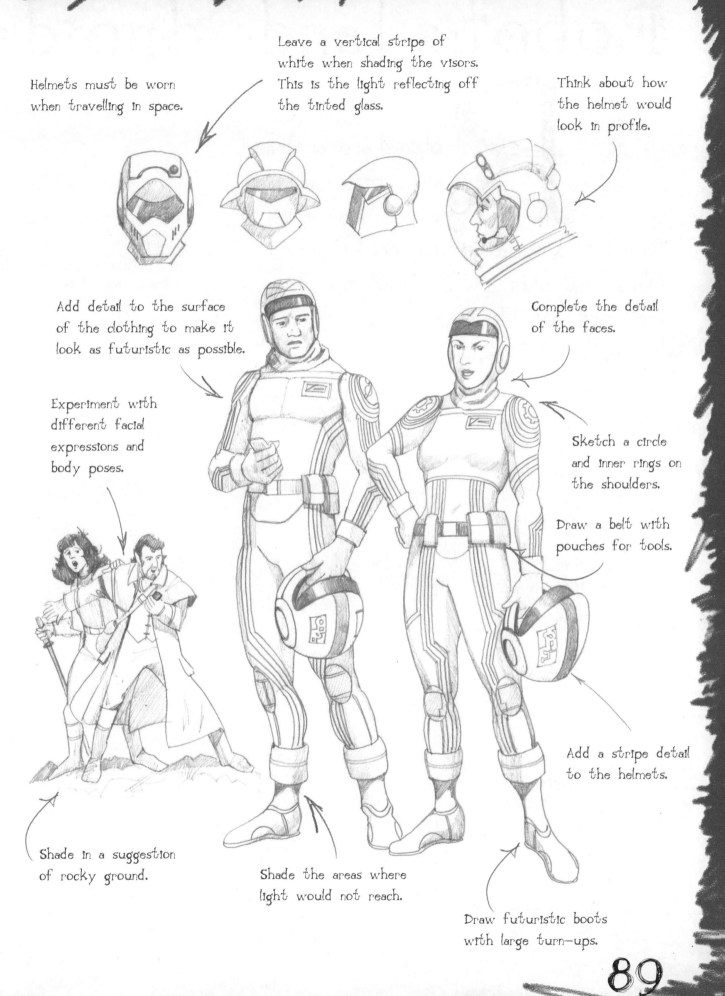

Helmets must be worn when travelling in space.

Leave a vertical stripe of white when shading the visors. This is the light reflecting off the tinted glass.

Think about how the helmet would look in profile.

Add detail to the surface of the clothing to make it look as futuristic as possible.

Complete the detail of the faces.

Experiment with different facial expressions and body poses.

Sketch a circle and inner rings on the shoulders.

Draw a belt with pouches for tools.

Add a stripe detail to the helmets.

Shade in a suggestion of rocky ground.

Shade the areas where light would not reach.

Draw futuristic boots with large turn-ups.

Robots and droids

DRAW

Robots are artificial, electronic machines which are often found in science—fiction books and films. Androids are designed to look and act like humans and can be very intelligent.

This detail looks a little like a circuit board. Add some to your drawing to make it look more robotic.

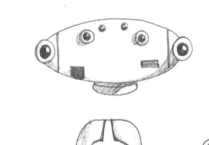

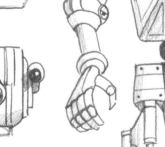

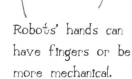

Robots' hands can have fingers or be more mechanical.

Try to make faces from unusual shapes. Use buttons, dials and switches.

Small circles can look like bolts that are holding the robot together.

Add dots and lines to the robot's metalwork to add interest.

Shade some areas where the light would not reach.

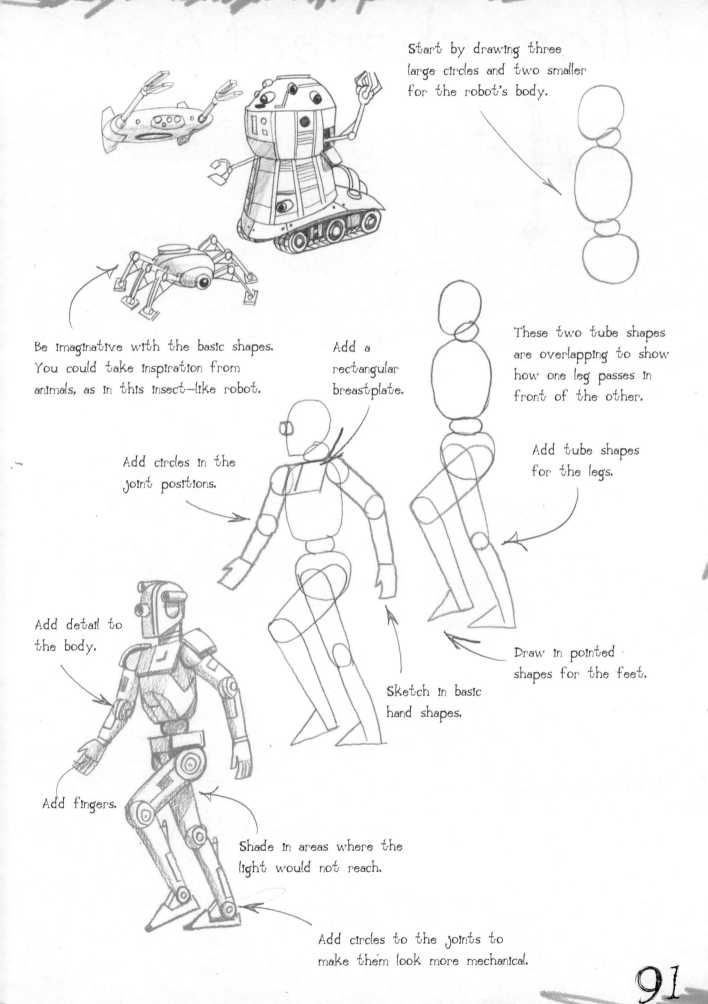

Start by drawing three large circles and two smaller for the robot's body.

Be imaginative with the basic shapes. You could take inspiration from animals, as in this insect-like robot.

Add a rectangular breastplate.

These two tube shapes are overlapping to show how one leg passes in front of the other.

Add circles in the joint positions.

Add tube shapes for the legs.

Add detail to the body.

Draw in pointed shapes for the feet.

Sketch in basic hand shapes.

Add fingers.

Shade in areas where the light would not reach.

Add circles to the joints to make them look more mechanical.

Alien characters

DRAW

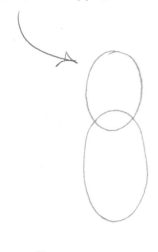

In science fiction, aliens are creatures that do not come from planet Earth. No-one knows what they really look like, so use your imagination to create your own crazy space alien.

Draw two ovals slightly overlapping.

Add snake-like shapes for tentacles.

Draw in two parallel lines for the base of the top oval.

Draw in some eyes on stalks and shade the oval to look like glass.

Sketch in branch-like shapes for the arms.

Add detail to the body.

Shade the areas where light would not reach.

Add a scaly pattern to the tentacles.

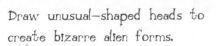

Draw unusual—shaped heads to create bizarre alien forms.

Some aliens have more than two eyes.

Add ferocious sharp teeth.

You could take inspiration from the feaures of dinosaurs.

Add darker parts of shading to the drawing for dramatic effect.

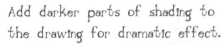

Add wing shapes.

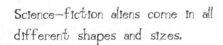

Science—fiction aliens come in all different shapes and sizes.

Stretch out arms and legs to make spidery alien body shapes.

93

Glossary

Chiaroscuro The practice of drawing high—contrast pictures with a lot of black and white, but not much grey.

Composition The arrangement of the parts of a picture on the drawing paper.

Construction lines Guidelines used in the early stages of a drawing. They are usually erased later.

Fixative A type of resin used to spray over a finished drawing to prevent smudging. **It should only be used by an adult.**

Focal point A central point of interest.

Light source The direction from which the light seems to come in a drawing.

Perspective A method of drawing in which near objects are shown larger than faraway objects to give an impression of depth.

Pose The position assumed by a figure.

Proportion The correct relationship of scale between each part of the drawing.

Silhouette A drawing that shows only a flat, dark shape, like a shadow.

Three—dimensional Having an effect of depth, so as to look lifelike or real.

Vanishing point The place in a perspective drawing where parallel lines appear to meet.

Index